More praise for
HOW TO WRITE A MYSTERY

"Larry Beinhart is a righteous Oxford Don. In this book is a post, post, post graduate course in writing great crime fiction. Anyone aspiring to write has to bring a native intelligence and talent to the place—but beyond that they have got to know the fundamental mystery writing form—Larry "The Don" Beinhart elucidates that form with great wit, precision and bedrock sensibility."
—James Ellroy

"Larry Beinhart is a wonderful writer. When he gives advice on writing mysteries, people would do well to listen."
—Sharyn McCrumb
New York Times bestselling author of
She Walks These Hills

"Larry Beinhart is a fine teacher, as his students at Oxford know. He is also a fine mystery writer, as his many happy readers know. Now he's combined his talents in a book that teaches you how to write the mystery. Whether you want to learn or just to read for pleasure, have I got a book for you."
—Donald Westlake

(*continued on next page*)

LARRY BEINHART

HOW TO WRITE A MYSTERY

BALLANTINE BOOKS, NEW YORK

Grateful acknowledgment is made to the following for permission to reprint previously published material:

Friends of New Mystery: Excerpts by Leslie Alan Horvitz from Reviews, *New Mystery*, Spring 1995, Vol. III, No. 2. Copyright 1995. Reprinted by permission of Friends of New Mystery.

Alfred A. Knopf, Inc.: Excerpts from *The Big Sleep* by Raymond Chandler. Copyright © 1939 by Raymond Chandler and renewed 1967 by Helga Greene, Executrix of the Estate of Raymond Chandler. Reprinted by permission of Alfred A. Knopf, Inc.

The New York Times: Excerpt from "Books of The Times: Mysteries that Reveal More than Just Whodunit" by Herbert Mitgang, August 7, 1992. Copyright © 1992 by The New York Times Company. Reprinted by permission of *The New York Times*.

Oxford University Press: Excerpts from *Concise Oxford Textbook of Psychiatry* by Michael Gelder, Dennis Gath, and Richard Mayou, 1994. Reprinted by permission of Oxford University Press.

Pocket Books and Lantz-Harris Literary Agency: Excerpt from *Alibi for an Actress* by Gillian B. Farrell. Copyright © 1992 by Gillian B. Farrell. Reprinted by permission of Pocket Books, a division of Simon & Schuster, and Lantz-Harris Literary Agency.

The Putnam Publishing Group: Excerpts from *The Godfather* by Mario Puzo. Copyright © 1969 by Mario Puzo. Reprinted by permission of The Putnam Publishing Group.

The Putnam Publishing Group and John Johnson (Author's Agent) Limited: Excerpts from *Reflex* by Dick Francis, published by Putnam and Michael Joseph, London. Copyright © 1980 by Dick Francis. Reprinted by permission of The Putnam Publishing Group and John Johnson Limited.

http://www.randomhouse.com

LIBRARY OF CONGRESS CATALOGING IN PUBLICATION DATA
Beinhart, Larry.
How to write a mystery / Larry Beinhart.
p.   cm.
ISBN 0-345-39758-4
1. Detective and mystery stories—Authorship.   I. Title.
PN3377.5.D4B397   1996
808.3'872—dc20   96-3516

Text design by Fritz Metsch
Cover design and illustration by Kayley LeFaiver

Manufactured in the United States of America
First Edition: July 1996
10 9 8 7 6 5 4

This is dedicated to
Betty Glass (nee Loss)
and Jen Mendelsohn (nee Beinhart),
one my mother's sister,
the other my father's sister.
Strong, intelligent, articulate, and literate
women of great character.

CONTENTS

ACKNOWLEDGMENTS

First, a general nod of gratitude and respect to all the mystery, crime, and thriller writers that I read growing up and continue to read and expect to read every time I get on an airplane, need a mental vacation, or want a second-hand thrill or a trip to someplace that's a little too far to go at the moment. There are some really, really great writers out there.

Specifically, I need to thank Joy Harris for selling it. Clare Ferraro for buying it. Cathy Repetti for making remarkably useful comments considering she is an editor. Also Joe Brady, J. Madison Davies, Justin Scott, Steve Womack, John DeSantis, Tim Binyon, Gillian Farrell, all of whom read earlier drafts and were kind enough to point out exactly how lacking they were. This version is vastly improved by their vile, unrelenting, virtually unendurable honesty. I thank them with more sincerity than I could ever speak with a straight face.

Gallagher Gray, Jeff Abbott, Steve Womack, Bill Bernhardt, Gillian Farrell, and Justin Scott were kind enough to share their writing ideas and experiences with me and allow me to use their opinions.

The Joy of Genre

Genre is a gaudy, tawdry Muse, but the favors she brings the writer are gifts of genuine gold.

The first and most important gift is—an Audience. It is from them that all the other gifts flow.

Like news, or for that matter, pornography, the audience is insatiable. Who could imagine that there could be more news programming? But there is. Or more skin magazines? But there are. Why are all those books in the mystery section and how come there are new ones every week? There are people who read a mystery a week, a day, or more. Personally, I never get on a plane, a train, a bus, or a subway without one.

That means that there is a Market.

Publishers need product, and quite a lot of it, to fill that market. If you can produce the material, almost regardless of

quality—it does not have to be the great American novel—
you can sell it.

This is a wonderful thing.

HOPE FOR THE WRITER

It's really intimidating to sit down at the keyboard with aspi-
rations of being Hemingway or Shakespeare. When I think
about someone doing that, his head full of Literature 101
Dreams of Immortality, I get a cartoon vision of a floor
littered with wads of crushed first pages—hundreds and
hundreds of them, decades of litter, not one page one good
enough to be the first page of a novel by the new James
Joyce.

> *The average detective novel is probably no worse than
> the average novel, but you never see the average novel. It
> doesn't get published. The average—or only slightly above
> average—detective story does. Not only is it published but
> it is sold . . . and it is read. . . .*
> Raymond Chandler, *The Simple Art of Murder*

The event that inspired me to become a working writer
was reading two truly dreadful mysteries in one day. There
and then I was convinced that if I wrote one, no matter how
bad it was, I could sell it.

It wasn't that I thought that I could do better. What was
exciting, thrilling, illuminating, was that someone had published these meandering, illogical, poorly constructed, cliché-
ridden manuscripts and—I presumed—actually paid the
writers! This was attainable.

When I tell this story I am always asked: Which two books
were they? I honestly don't remember. But I have certainly

read many since then that are just as bad or worse. If someone else feels a book inside them, but needs the same sort of
perverse incitement to write it, there are lots of terrible
books out there. In any case, that gave me the courage and
the self-confidence to write a first page, keep it, get past it,
write a second page, and on and on, until there was a complete manuscript. Which I duly brought to an agent who
sold it to a publisher who printed it and put it in bookstores
which sold it. To people rather like me.

This is not meant to imply, in any way, that I, or other authors, do less than their best, or that they write down, or that
it's easy. Like the other authors I know, I always try to write
the best book I can. At times it's very difficult. It is meant to
say that the goal is in reach. If you can write a clear sentence,
if you can organize your thoughts, if you know the field and
love it, and if you will make the commitment, you can probably write a salable book.

WHAT IS GENRE?

The simplest, most effective, and laziest definition is that it's
whatever gets you placed on the mystery rack rather than
with general fiction.

However, there are those novels that escape the ghetto
and move over to the main shelves and even to the "hot"
book table at the front of the store, that don't seem any different than the ones in the crime section. Actually, at any
given time, a minimum of half the books on the bestseller
lists are mysteries or detective novels or thrillers or legal
thrillers. For their sake, let us throw in a second simple definition: they are books that have, as their center, the commission of a crime or the discovery of who committed a
crime.

AND WHY THERE IS A MARKET

The basic story of the mystery genre is "whodunit." There are, of course, endless variations, alterations, and decorations, howdunit, whydunit, whatcha gonna do about it, but "whodunit" is the essence.

It is a matter of human nature that once a question is raised, people want the matter settled. In other words, if you kill someone on page one and pose the question "whodunit?" a fair number of people will stay with you long enough to find out the answer.

If we liken a book to a train, the "puzzle" is the engine. A nongenre writer has to invent an engine—create a question that people will want answered—and then convince a potential audience that it is a train, that it will take them on the sort of journey they like, and they therefore ought to give it a try. The genre writer gets this for free: the audience knows it's a train, that it has an engine that will make it go, and that it is, more or less, the sort of journey they like.

> *Opening with a riddle frees the author from the frequently demanding task of drawing his readers into the narrative by other means. . . . Knowing that a book is a thriller guarantees a plot: it promises an element of entertainment so often lacking in the "serious" novel.*
> Piers Paul Read, the *Times*, September 16, 1995

It's a train. People get on. The qualitative questions come afterward: Did you give them a good ride? How was the scenery and how were the companions?

The answer to the first—did you roar on through? keep on chugging? run out of steam? jump off the tracks?—separates the successful from the unsuccessful.

The answers to the last two—how vivid were the views?

did your riders-readers make new friends? or did they have to endure shallow bores mouthing the old clichés they'd heard on previous journeys? was the dialogue lively and picaresque?—those are the things that separate the truly good from the merely mechanical.

When it's a really good railroad, the passengers don't care where the train goes. Most readers of Ian Fleming and John Le Carré have no independent interest in real-life espionage. Most readers of Dick Francis have no interest in horse racing, and even less in the esoteric variant which most of his books are about—steeple chasing.

So as long as you kill somebody in chapter one and tell 'em whodunit at the end, you get to pick the territory. In other words, your job is to explore and write about things that interest you until you get bored with them, and then you can find something new to work into a crime story. Tony Hillerman is obviously fascinated with Native American life and lore. In *Daughter of Time* it is absolutely clear that Josephine Tey was delighted by the deceptions of history. James Ellroy's mother was murdered when he was young. The police didn't solve the mystery. Ellroy, obsessed by it, found the time and the money to investigate it thirty years after the event, by turning it into a book proposal. Robert Parker likes to cook and he likes clothes, and these interests fill up a lot of the Spenser books. Eric Ambler filled his books with the politics of Mediterranean, Near Eastern, and Eastern European countries. Gerald Seymour, like a war reporter, goes wherever people are killing each other in the name of God and country. There are books set in suburban dental offices, on boats at sea, in late-twentieth-century Cleveland, in alternate realities in which Hitler won World War II, and in a future in which the uneasy buddy relationship is between a human cop from earth and an android cop from the outer worlds. I like to ski, so I set a novel in the

Austrian resort of St. Anton and had to spend six solid weeks skiing there to research it.

A lot of readers want an informative, fact-filled tour. Info-tainment. Recreation that is actually education. Who can feel that they're wasting their time with a trashy detective novel while tracking the medieval arcana of Umberto Eco's *The Name of the Rose*?

Herbert Mitgang, who writes about all types of literature, not *merely* mysteries, for the *New York Times*, put it this way in a review of two books, Walter Mosley's *White Butterfly* and Gillian Farrell's *Alibi for an Actress*:

> While taking the reader for a ride before solving the mystery, the best writers in the field have something to say about a city, a profession, a just cause, a moral climate. Of course, the detective story must abide by the rules of pursuit and solution. But it doesn't violate the formula if, lurking between the lines, there's a novel of manners, mostly bad.

In the article quoted earlier, Piers Paul Read, a *serious* writer, was actually being defensive about writing a thriller. This was in England, where they are actually still quite serious about the distinction between real writers and popular writers. Using the genre conventions, he went on to say:

> . . . The reader, comfortably seated, is happy to enjoy the landscape as the story hurtles along. . . . [The author] can treat his loftier themes in passing: in this case . . . history, iconography, patriotism, consumerism, communism, feminism and love. [There, are these serious and correct enough for you?!]

PLAYING THE GAME

In many ways, writing in a genre is like a sport, you do the same thing over and over. It's something other people are doing, that people have done before you and will do after you. Yet each single game is specific, unique, and individual, as well as good, bad, or mediocre.

The rules of the game are more in the nature of mores (or mythos or folklore) than they are a matter of statute. There is no place where they are written down. When someone does it wrong, we don't say he or she is in violation of N.Y. Literary Code 33.247, we simply feel that it's wrong. The rules aren't the same for everybody. As with all matters of sensibility and etiquette, some people can get away with murder, and some people can't.

The game itself is largely one of cleverness. This is most obviously true in the traditional cozy, aka the "fair play mystery," in which the author presents the same clues both to the reader and to the fictional detective. The reader tries to guess, from those clues, whodunit and how. The puzzle, and therefore the book, is good if, strictly from those clues, the fictional detective can figure out the case but the reader can't. No matter how far we move from this rather antiquated style, the underlying principle remains valid. When we, the readers, figure something out before the detective does, we get irritated and bored and lose respect for him. We are up ahead at the conclusion, the idiot is stuck in a muddle somewhere behind us, and until he catches up, the story lags unbearably.

A lot more of today's writing has moved to the thriller side of the continuum. Over there the hero is in danger as he attempts to solve the problem. The writer's ingenuity is then applied to putting the hero in an impossible situation and coming up with a way out of it that's so smart that the reader didn't think of it first. This resourcefulness need not take a cerebral form. The hero may solve the case by allowing himself to be beaten beyond the limits of human endurance, since one of his qualities, unknown to the villain, is to have a pain threshold so high that it would leave the Marquis de Sade crying his heart out from frustration.

Certain things have been done in the past. If they work, they're imitated. It's easy to say they're tired old clichés. But it's not that simple. A good chess opening lives on and on. So does a good mystery opening. The practices, techniques, formations, and tactics of soccer, football, baseball, tennis, have multigenerational life spans—if they work. They usually evolve slowly. When they die a sudden death, someone usually brings them back in a new form a few years later.

A writer can stick with the good old moves, the tried and true. Let's call this *formula*.

Here again the comparison with sex and news is apt. The occasional bit of erotica that can be marketed into the mainstream makes more money than porn. But people who are interested enough in sex to buy its representation on a regular basis (in a capitalist society that's the definition of an audience) are quite satisfied with a picture or description of a body part and its function. For them depth of meaning and aesthetic eminence don't matter. So porn remains and hasn't been replaced by "erotica." As television channels multiply, news programming expands even more rapidly. From time to time someone takes a shot at adding depth and insight, only to rediscover that improving the product in that way does not guarantee an increase in market share. Titillation, scandal, and fear-mongering are reliable sellers. The quality of reporting is not elevated, tabloid standards and headline news proliferate.

In books, too, formula, and virtually nothing but the formula, may indeed be where it's at. Several of the top-selling crime writers do exactly that: formula—with nothing else.

This is not to say that writing formula so well that you can get rich from it is easy. It's not. It's hard. And the people who can do it reliably, over and over again, are rare indeed. There are one or two of them whose work I look forward to all year. When I get one of their books I want to go off and read it with a sensual anticipation similar to settling down alone with a whole container of Häagen-Dazs.

Far more often, formula books don't reach this standard. Then, as an audience member, I find them to be, at best, unsatisfying, frequently irritating, and, at worst, unreadable. As a writer, I don't want to write that way.

HAVING FUN & MAKING OLD THINGS NEW

One of the simplest and most effective ways to freshen up the genre is to put the hero in a dress.

The hero of American fiction and of detective fiction has been the same person who owns the country—the adult white (vaguely Episcopal and certainly heterosexual) male. You can take an old Ross Macdonald novel and make the hero a heroine (Sue Grafton) and you have an entirely new product. You can take an old Ross Macdonald novel and redo it with a gay hero (Joseph Hansen) and you have an entirely new product. You can take a Raymond Chandler novel, make Philip Marlowe a Jewish hippie, or an African-American, or a Chicano—same story, same machinations, same tour of characters and places, same type of denouement—and you have a new product.

This can be a gimmick or a true revitalization of a tired format. The difference is this: If it's a gimmick, nothing else changes; if it's a true renewal of the genre, then the perspective changes, the dialogue freshens up, the dynamic between the characters is different. Surely if I were a suspect, I would react differently to being questioned by John Shaft or Kinsey Milhone or Moses Wine than the way I used to react in the old days when it was Sam Spade grilling me.

In terms of salability, the gimmick may be enough. But I like to think that one of the reasons that Tony Hillerman is so successful is that Jim Chee is not just Miss Marple on the reservation. We enter a different world with different perceptions, different ways of interacting, of observing, and of thinking.

We can alter the time. What I set out to do in my first novel—very explicitly—was to update my old favorites. I literally asked myself the question "What would Sam Spade be like in the seventies, the age of ambiguity, instead of the twenties?" Lindsey Davis took a similar character and tossed him back to the first century A.D., when he knocks around the mean streets of Rome. Minette Walters brought fresh life to the cozy by dragging it into the present. She gave it a feminist sensibility, depicting the relationships between men and women in terms of power, and put in really kinky sexual relationships.

Change of locale can perform the same function. The mildly eccentric founder of Murder Ink, one of New York's mystery bookshops, thought place was so important to the genre and to the readers that she organized the store by the geographic location of the detective's office, not alphabetically by author's name. There was a time, and it's not entirely gone, when hard-boiled PI novels were set in either California or New York, and cozies were set in English villages. Putting the hero in Florida, like Travis McGee, was a major innovation.

Again, this can be a gimmick, like going to a shoot on location to get pretty pictures in the background and giving a few happy natives bit parts. But places are more than just different spots on a map and local color for the tourists. They are where life is actually different, like James Lee Burke's Louisiana, Paco Taibo III's Mexico City, or Michael Dibdin's Italy.

Another way to play with a genre is the technique of inversion.

I learned inversion from George Bernard Shaw. He wrote in a period when the stage play was what television is now, the primary form of populist entertainment. It was full of genres: farces, melodramas, tragedies, romantic comedies, the way TV today has sitcoms, docudramas, MOWs, and action shows. All it takes is just two or three minutes of watching a TV show to know pretty much who every character is, what their attitudes are, how they relate. We also know in what terms the story will be told, and in essence, how it will be resolved. Most of us can even, as my mother does when she watches, announce what the characters are about to do a moment or two before they do it. In Shaw's day, the theater was a lot like that. He was able to be fresh and totally original by using stock characters and stock situations and simply inverting the audience's expectation.

In *Arms and the Man* the heroic cavalry officer of noble blood—he probably looks like Richard Gere—turns out to be a shallow dimwit, suited only for posing for portraits. The beautiful heroine chooses the apparently cowardly, money-grubbing bourgeois, the Danny DeVito character. *Mrs. Warren's Profession* is about a prostitute. There were then, as there are now, three kinds of cliché whores: the heart of gold, the pathetic (dies for her sins), and the merry (often has a euphemistic title like "dance hall girl"). Shaw made Mrs. Warren a hardheaded businessperson without shame or regret. In *Man and Superman* the ingenue is revealed as absolutely ruthless in her genetic drive to snare the best husband. In Shaw's day the munitions maker was as reliable a dastard as the real estate developer of the eighties and the kiddie porn dealer of the nineties. In *Major Barbara* Shaw makes him a figure of intelligence, vibrancy, and moral leadership. The young hero chooses to abandon Art and go off to build cannons.

Joseph Heller's *Catch-22* is *the* great comic inversion novel. World War II is a genre all to itself. This five-year period generated more clichés than all the mystery novels in history combined. Virtually every one of Heller's characters, every gag, every bit of business, and the plot itself is an inversion of the conventions established by its predecessors.

This would imply that inversion is largely a comic technique. It's not. *The Spy Who Came In from the Cold* was a kind of inversion novel, pitting realism against myth. Without discounting its brilliance, its impact at the time was so very intense because it was written in a genre completely dominated by James Bond and his imitators—glamorous, successful, violent agents who had Pussy Galore. Le Carré's novel was a sudden film noir after a decade of color cartoons.

It's quite possible to have a book that is, overall, conventional, but in which inversion is used for specific characters and specific scenes. In Bob Leuci's *Fence Jumpers*, the hero, a white male heterosexual cop, has a thing for his partner, a white female almost certainly lesbian cop. They do end up in bed together. If James Bond had been involved, she would have gotten the bonking she needed, and been converted in midorgasm. In Leuci's book she rubs his back, comforts him, grows closer to him, does not have sex with him, and stays gay. It's sad, funny, and fresh.

As in the western, one of the stock characters in a mystery is the crusty-but-lovable old sidekick. Part of his job is to get killed, or at least severely injured. This has two functions: to show how really bad the bad guys are, and to give the hero a crisis of conscience, since it was the hero's activities, however well intended, that have brought pain and suffering to this great old guy. In my first novel I had such a character. I had reached a point in the story that called for me to get the dear old fellow out of the way. My villains were *drug kingpins*, the evilest thing in creation that decade, so they were standing by, ready and willing. And it was also time for my hero to experience a severe setback. But it was terribly expected and I felt weary just thinking about it. Instead, I gave the guy a heart attack. This changed the whole dynamic. It permitted the subsequent scene to be lively and comic, in a black humor sort of way, instead of being turgid, angst ridden, and exactly what was expected.

Although a book appears to be a monologue, writing is a dialogue between author and reader. This body of knowledge, this experience of the genre, which the writer shares with the reader, makes it easier for the conversation to take place. In many ways it defines the language in which the conversation takes place. And it permits this kind of playing.

THE VITALITY OF THE GENRE

One of the most exciting pieces of writing about writing that I've ever read is Tom Wolfe's introduction to the collection he edited called *The New Journalism* (Harper & Row, 1972).

The essence of it—or one of the essences—was that the novel used to have a job to do—to show us how other people lived. Having a job gave the novel vigor and made the novelist an important person. He or she was the guide, the explorer, the reporter, the teacher of unknown things, foreign and domestic. Wolf felt that the job had been abdicated: "The most serious, ambitious and, presumably, talented novelist had abandoned the richest terrain of the novel: namely, society, the social tableau, manners and morals, the whole business of 'the way we live now,'. . . . That was marvelous for journalists." The journalists took up new positions and occupied the abandoned territory.

Alternatively, it might be said that the job had been supplanted by journalism, just as photography had taken reportage away from painters, and that novelists had retreated to minimalism and academicism, just as painters had retreated to abstract expressionism and other movements that concerned themselves with form for the sake of form. Henceforth, Wolfe suggested, the new Great American Novels would be works of the Great American New Journalists.

Wolfe went on to fulfill his own prophecy, writing works of nonfiction that rivaled or surpassed most books of fiction in exactly the realms that belonged to the novelist—image, phrase making, dialogue, stylization, character creation, drama, and plot. He did so in lengths that matched everything from the short story to the Dickensian novel. After that, he went and wrote a novel that did all those things that he said the novel had abdicated. When Wolfe finally did write that novel, *Bonfire of the Vanities*, it was a crime novel.

The crime novel, unlike the mainstream novel, has never given up its functions—to entertain and to tour. Take me where I can't go, teach me something about what it means to be someone I can't be: an African-American (Chester Himes), homosexual (Joseph Hansen), a South African under apartheid (James McClure), an Englishman when the Empire has fallen (John Le Carré), a Russian as Communism totters (Martin Cruz Smith), a small-time hood in Boston (George Higgins), an L.A. cop (Joseph Wambaugh). Teach me what it means to live in your world—the sounds and smells, the biology, the fears and the pains, the lies and relationships, the money and politics.

•　　•　　•　　•

There are other views of what the genre is. Someone else taking an overview would have referred to a very different list of books. I've probably made it appear that mystery novels are full of politics, exotic locales, and intense issues.

In fact, the bulk of genre material, in books or television, tends to have a very narrow vision. It excludes, for the most part, sex, politics, race, money, and religion. Except as titillation, of course. It expresses, for the most part, what George Bernard Shaw used to call "conventional morality," and an unquestioning view of the world. There are more detective heroines named Cat (or Kat) than there are African-American crime writers. There are probably more cats in mystery novels than African-American characters. Detectives seem to need no visible means of support, and lack of money is never a plot issue. I don't know that I've ever read a crime novel that endorsed genuinely treasonous political views.

There are people who say quite frankly that this is the way it should be. There are readers and writers who feel that the appeal of crime fiction is escapism to a world in which

> *they are reassured from the start knowing that the criminal will be caught, an orderly path to being caught will be laid, and punishment meted out, whether by man or by fate. . . .*
> *The average mystery reader does not want sex. Sex gets in the way of a good plot progression. Though romance is very satisfying. . . . [And the reader] hates, detests and absolutely* loathes *political lectures in crime novels.*
>
> Gallagher Gray

I know editors who agree. In the chapter on sex you'll find the passage over which I had a fight with an editor at Crown. *American Hero* was initially turned down by an editor who believed that political satire didn't sell. And when it was published, some of the mystery bookstore owners, very important people in our business, did treat it as if I had moved off the reservation. Another editor didn't care what I wrote, as long as I kept my series going.

This is not surprising if we remember that not very long ago the mainstays of this business were Agatha Christie, Sherlock Holmes, The Saint, Perry Mason, and Nero Wolfe.

What I prefer to believe is that as long as you do what they did—create a compulsively readable story that a publisher in good conscience can call a mystery or thriller or crime novel—then you can *also* do whatever else you want. You can cover any subject. You can write in a variety of styles. You can be escapist or you can rub the reader's face in the rawest realism you can find. You can be complicated or simple. The hero can be a cop, a killer, or a member of a baby group.

It's a mansion with many rooms.

CHAPTER 1

Narrative Drive

NARRATIVE DRIVE #1

Narrative Drive is what sells books. To agents, publishers, readers. We all know near-illiterate, insultingly dumb books that (a) have made the bestseller list to our incredulous envy, and (b) have had us reading them even as we say to ourselves, "My God, why am I reading this brain-damaged idiocy?!"

What is narrative drive? The best way to discover narrative drive is to read material that you can't put down, but you don't know why. It should not have literary merit (whatever that is) or have real and fascinating characters or be informative about subjects that interest you.

The first time I remember having this reaction was while reading Harold Robbins. When I lectured about this at Oxford, one of my students told me that she had just experienced the My-God-why-am-I-reading-this syndrome with a

Patricia Cornwell novel. Year after year, Dick Francis tells the same story, with the same hero, in the same way. All he changes is the horse. Yet every time a new one comes out I can't wait to read it. Other people might feel this way about John Grisham, Robert Parker, Elmore Leonard, Agatha Christie, and Conan Doyle. If you don't agree and feel that Grisham has great insights into the subconscious paranoias of the American psyche and that Leonard's gift for dialogue and capsule characterization lifts him to the level of literature, that's fine. Make your own choices of writers whose work can keep you up reading, but after spending the night with them, you don't respect yourself in the morning.

Also, look at TV soap operas. Nowhere is the addiction to narration, empty of substance or grace, made more vivid.

Narrative drive is the promise—or threat or tease or suggestion—that *something is going to happen*.

There are apparent variations on this: something has happened and we are going to *reveal the secret, uncover the culprit, find the truth*. This is the same thing in disguise. Revelation-is-imminent is a something-that-is-going-to-happen. In stage plays, as a result of their physical limitations, the most important action is, more often than not, a revelation. As Oedipus used to say: "You're my *what?*"

Soap operas are fascinating. Virtually nothing ever happens. What does happens takes so long to unfold that it is the only art form that moves slower than real time. Yet viewers are more than fans, they are addicts. The key is in the structure, and the structure is the constant promise that something is going to happen.

Horror films are also instructive. Even cursory viewing reveals that much more time is spent on things almost happening than actually happening. We will jump under our seats when the victim turns the corner into the dark and the monster is *not there*. A typical horror film rhythm is: We think he's there. *Not there.* We think he's there. *Not there.* We think he's there. *Not there.* We think he's there. It's got to be this time because there've been so many false alarms. *Not there.* OK. He's not here. Bang! *He's here.*

The point is not how many times the monster is not there—the point is the constant promise that *an action is going to happen.*

Action can be a misleading word. It makes us think of shoot-outs, car chases, explosions. Go back to soap operas. Here the promised actions are things like—they will go to bed, she will tell a lie, he will embezzle funds, she will find out her real father is an alien, she will let a crucial slip slip, he will mistakenly believe, and so on. Sometimes we have to explain why the matter is important: if Caren tells Susie that Fred is seeing Lisa, Susie will distrust Fred (who is a good guy and truly loves Susie) and reject Fred (miss out on true love and a good guy) and fall prey to Ted, a lying, scheming louse who doesn't even want her for her splendid body and blue eyes, but to hurt her in order to gain revenge on her father.

Narrative drive is *something is going to happen and it matters.*

NARRATIVE DRIVE #2

When an actor analyzes a scene he tries to figure out: What does the character want in this scene? What does the character want in each line?

What does the character want can also be expressed as: Where does he want to get to? What is his objective? The attempt to get somewhere or get something or achieve a goal animates the scene. Without that, the scene becomes a diorama, one of those static still lifes at the American

Museum of Natural History with a stuffed buffalo in the foreground and a big sky painted on a curved wall behind it.

In a typical mystery the protagonist is *seeking the truth*.

Sometimes this is enough. Other times it is necessary to add weight and gravity to the search. Therefore, we construct a situation in which the wrong person will go to the electric chair—soon—if the real culprit isn't found or the perpetrator will strike again or the victim must be avenged.

Here's the simple and basic scene. Sam, the protagonist detective, walks into a scene. The location is the house of Charles, character number one. Sam wants the truth. Charles, who is in a position to know important and vital things, wants to be left alone. The reason that Charles wants to be left alone, combined with his character and capabilities, will determine how that is expressed. Let's say that he has some personal peculiarities that would be revealed in the course of such an investigation. He says: "You don't have any authority. Go away." Quite right, too.

This is the typical and most basic problem the investigator faces—why should anyone talk to him? That's an obstacle. Now Sam has to figure out how to get through, over, or around the Obstacle. Typically Sam threatens Charles. But with what? How about: "Talk to me or talk to the police. Whichever way you want it."

Charles is a man of substance and assurance. He says: "Screw you, good-bye, my lawyer will talk to the police."

End of scene. Obstacle insurmountable.

Now there is a new goal. To find something that will make Charles talk.

You should be able to make a simple sketch of each scene. Draw an arrow. It points where the character wants to go. Draw a line or a lump right in front of the arrow. That's an obstacle. What does that do to the arrow? Stop it? Deflect it? Send it on a detour? Make the character shoot harder to break through the lump?

Each person in the scene has a different goal. They may even have more than one. To get the truth and, at the same time, to bring a romantic relationship to consummation. The goal may change in midscene—say, from investigating to escaping. But every action and every sentence should have a goal.

A character should not say hello unless he intends to achieve something with that hello. As in: I greeted him with a cheery hello, to disguise the fear and shame I felt.

Each obstacle creates a subgoal that must be achieved to get to the main goal. The overall plot becomes this linked series of movements: toward goal, deflection, toward the subgoal, deflection, toward the new subgoal, and so on, until the climax where we are at the goal again.

NARRATIVE DRIVE #3

It is focus that turns activity into action.

If activity is focused on a goal, it can be about things that seem inconsequential. You can proceed slowly. It will allow you room to play.

You must make it clear to yourself why someone must get to where he is going, what he will gain by it, what he will lose if he fails. Most of the time you must make it just as clear to the reader. The exception being when you are withholding information for effect.

When an electrical device doesn't work, the first thing you should do is to check to see if it is plugged in. If a scene lies flat, the first thing to check is if you have made these three things clear—where the characters are trying to go, what can be won, what may be lost.

A lot of activity is not a lot of action. Adding more activity does not create a greater sense of action or more attention on the part of the reader. More focus will create the feeling of more action. Frequently with less activity.

NARRATIVE DRIVE #4

Sports have great narrative drive. That is the essence of why we watch them, read about them, and follow them: Who will win? Will our heroes overcome the opposition and reach their goal? Will their play be sharp and creative or clumsy and dull?

Sports are virtually subjectless. They are about nothing but themselves.

Though sportswriters may laden them with talk about morality and economics and philosophy and politics, we do not watch for any of those reasons. We watch for the intensity of the contest and for the level of skill brought to it.

There is lots of talk about the personalities and the private lives of sports figures. This might create the illusion that those are the things we care about. We don't. At least not very much. No one would have cared that John McEnroe's court conduct was "bratty" if he hadn't been a tennis player of such brilliance that he spent much of his career at or near the number one spot in the world. Now that Mac is gone, the press fills the sports columns with Agassi's wardrobe. Mike Tyson's personal life would be just another five minutes on an overcrowded criminal court calendar except for how fast his fists move and how hard they hit.

For the most part our interest derives from our fascination with the contest. We care about the "color" and the details and the fascinating anecdotes precisely in proportion to the excitement of the pennant race or the drive to the play-offs or race to the championship.

This tells us that it is not subject matter that creates narrative drive. It is not character. It is not style. It is not anything "literary." It is orientation toward the goal and the force of the opposition that creates narrative drive.

CHAPTER 2

Plotting

Plotting—the organization of the story—is an exercise in logic more than of imagination. At least the craft of plotting is.

The craft of plotting is the sequential arrangement of materials—information and events. Events are those things in which characters participate that result in uncovering information. They then engage in new actions that reveal more material. The substance—the psychopathology of crime, the clash of subcultures in New York, the economics of horse racing, the rage of love—may be a matter of imagination or of research or of knowledge, but putting it together is an exercise in logic.

Certain things cause other things. Causal events must precede effects. Knowledge is a causal event. Discovery must precede the effects of discovery. Certain actions will be committed only in ignorance. I would inform the killer of the progress of my investigation only if I don't know he is the killer. I will accuse the innocent suspect only if I don't know she was in bed with her husband's sister at the time of the murder. Once a person knows something, he will act in a different way. Knowledge must be dispensed and withheld to control what characters do.

In its most primitive sense it is simply that certain things must precede other things. The client must hire the PI before he begins his quest. The similarity in the MO of a serial killer must come to the attention of a police agency before he is investigated as a serial killer.

The investigator will have tools, limitations, and a certain amount of information. The small-town cop, the professional PI, the head of an FBI major crime unit, a fantasy secret avenger/equalizer/superhero, the amateur investigator, all have different capabilities and resources. These determine things they are capable of and things that they are not.

Having constructed a crime, having determined what evidence there might be—based on a combination of logic and your convenience, since you're making it up—you begin with what your hero is capable of doing in that situation.

The next step is for the investigator to make a choice from the things that he is capable of. That decision will be based on the person's "character," his professional and his personal priority systems, possibly in conflict, the pressures placed on him, and so on.

Each step forward both enables and eliminates.

Imagine a map, a huge complicated one, like a road map of the United States. You're in St. Louis. You're searching for something. You don't know where it is. You start your journey and you head . . . where? East. You now have a whole section of the country behind you. As you travel, you have to decide which way to go. Each turn opens up new possibilities, but more or less eliminates others. The farther you go, the harder it is to get back. I forgot to mention, you're traveling by bicycle, you don't have plane fare, and the killer you're looking for selects his victims from among hitchhikers. So if you've cycled down to Nashville, you've pretty well eliminated Jackson Hole, Wyoming, as your next stop. Also, in order to get to certain places, there are others you absolutely must go through. To get from St. Louis, Missouri, to Nashville, Tennessee, you have to cross the Mississippi, and unless you head straight south before you head east, you have to cross the Ohio River. To bring someone to trial in New York State the prosecution must first have sufficient evidence to convince a grand jury to hand up an indictment. In England the police must have enough evidence to convince a Crown Prosecutor to bring the case. That isn't necessarily a lot, but it is some. And they are required stopping points on the journey.

There are two plot structures: The Journey and The Contest.

Like all good, clear, simple statements, that's not entirely true. Exceptions, alternatives, variations, shadings, and combinations immediately come to mind. However, it is true enough, especially as a concept to work with,—that is to say, a tool.

The Journey is structurally the simpler of the two.

The hero has a problem, most typically to discover whodunit. The end, the goal, is the solution. There are difficulties in this journey.

When I think of a Mickey Spillane novel I visualize it as a hero going in a straight line, smashing through a series of brick walls.

I would visualize the structure of a Hercule Poirot story as a maze.

John Le Carré's George Smiley picks his way through a maze on top of a minefield. He moves slowly, carefully, since with a misstep someone gets blown up.

The classical journey story is Homer's *Odyssey*. Computer games—and lots of crime novels—have the same structure. The hero goes from one wildly different environment to another. Each time he has to figure out what the new place is like: what are the dangers; who is the enemy; who are his allies, if any; which of his powers are useful; what should he take with him when he leaves; and, finally, how does he get out and on to the next difficult, dangerous, devious environment.

In the course of his journey home Odysseus finds himself in the Land of the Lotus Eaters; he encounters the Cyclops; is betrayed by his own men; meets Circe the enchantress, who turns men into animals; visits the shades of the dead; sails past the Sirens and then between Scylla and Charybdis; encounters storms, shipwrecks, tempests; has arguments with the gods and a couple of other relationships with women. A detective hero might begin in the boardroom, then go to the police, then to the mean streets to meet his informant, where he is betrayed, but he escapes to a crack house, then goes to a bedroom, where a Circe turns him into a pig. When he gets away from her he falls in with a religious cult, where his life is threatened in the name of a god, but he escapes after a boat chase through a dangerous channel with cliffs on both sides. When he gets to shore he has a fistfight with a giant, followed by a gun battle. He survives, by the grace of a god, but he's injured and has to be nursed by some really cute nurses. It's hard to leave them, but he's a responsible kind of guy, so he goes "home" only to find that the bad guys have taken over while he was away. He infiltrates his own home, in disguise, takes the bad guys by surprise, and slaughters them.

If we were all assigned to write a New Odyssey, we would each come up with different equivalents of those events. The variations would arise automatically out of each author's tastes, inclinations, and knowledge. As soon as the basic choices are made, a thousand other details are suggested, or eliminated, by the nature of the story and the kind of world in which it takes place. If I make my Odysseus a Dublin Jew, I have a very different set of scenes than if he is a black Los Angeles football player.

The cozy usually takes place in a single world, and a quite circumscribed one at that, inhabited by a limited number of people of relatively narrow social range. The hard-boiled detective, like Philip Marlowe, is more likely to go from the bottom to the top of society and into the nooks and crannies of subcultures. But either kind of investigation can be seen as a simple journey.

Wherever the journey goes, the point of it is the discovery or uncovering or revelation of information. Even when the thriller has an Orgy of Violence finale, the end is still about the Revelation of the Truth.

The Contest is between two opponents.

It's possible to make it more complex than that and have three or four or more. For example, a treasure-hunt sort of plot, with hordes of people after the prize. Or when the hero has both the cops and the mob after him. The structure doesn't change, it just becomes somewhat more complicated, so I'll discuss it as though there were only two sides.

The structure can be thought of like a sporting event, though since it's a written report of the events, it has the feel of the sports commentator's version of the events rather than of the events themselves. Part of the announcer's job is to dramatize, and part of the way he dramatizes is by describing the abilities and the limitations that each side brings to the contest. That's exactly what the novelist does. Each move gives one side or the other an edge. The other side makes a countermove.

These moves are frequently made in ignorance of each other, though each side may have an idea of the sort of move that the opposition is likely to make in the situation. The defense in American football will try to anticipate what play the offense will choose. The serial killer is the offense. He will try to score. Scoring is killing. The defense will try—based on experience, intuition, and a knowledge of the possible offenses—to block the killer from his goal. More than that, they will try to get through the metaphorical screen of linesmen and confusion and deception and take the quarterback out of the game.

A perfect example of the contest novel is Thomas Harris's *Red Dragon*, the quintessential Serial Killer vs. FBI Expert novel. The other one that's as good is also his, *The Silence of the Lambs*.

Another useful image of the structure is what the early moviemakers used to call the race of the Train and the Model T. The Train is carrying the villain. The Hero is in the car. If the Hero can get to the station first, he has a chance to stop the villain. If not, the bad guy gets away with the gold, the girl, and the deed to the ranch. The road crosses the track. Several times. The car must get to the crossing first. Too late and the driver must wait so long that he will automatically lose the race. At the same time and he gets smashed. Too soon, of course, would be boring. So usually he gets across just in the nick of time.

In other words, the structure is a constant race to and through smash points. If the train is the Serial Killer and the Model T is the G-Man, the big smash points are when the killer will kill again and those occasions when the killer puts himself in a position to get caught.

The investigator moves forward by uncovering information. So does the villain.

> *All suspense novels . . . rely for their impact on the distribution of information. Who knows what when? If the hero knows something the villain does not there may not be much suspense at all; if on the other hand, the villain knows something the hero does not, we may be sitting on the edge of our seats in anticipation. Alternatively the reader . . . may be aware of some piece of information that neither hero nor villain have any way of knowing. . . . By placing us in such a privileged position [the author] allows us the pleasure of observing his characters suffer from delusions and misunderstandings, and then acting on them.*
> Leslie Alan Horvitz in a review of *The Day After Tomorrow* in *New Mystery Magazine* (Spring 1995, vol. III, no. 2)

There are two schematics of the plot: the visible one that the readers see and the invisible one that the author uses.

The real-life investigator may go plunging off into the rich chaos of reality where whatever happens happens. Not in fiction.

In effect, the author knows everything that the characters are going to find out. In fact, he probably knows a great deal more, since there are things that the writer never gets around to using. Or that get cut.

For example, in the cozy we usually have a situation in which there are a bunch of suspects who could have done it. They all have to have motive and opportunity and some alibi, which will or will not be verified. There should be clues that point to each. Then the writer arranges how the information will be doled out to the detective and in what order. That's the plot.

With that kind of setup a writer might want a chart. This is a working chart of the murder night created at one point during the writing of *Murder and a Muse*, by Gillian Farrell. In this story a film is being shot on location in a resort hotel off in the country. Alan, the director, is found dead in the bedroom of the heroine/investigator, Annie McGrogan. She had been contemplating an affair with him until his family showed up. Annie is, of course, the main suspect.

Alan's family consists of Angie, his ex-supermodel wife; Gavin, their son (old enough to kill); Chelsea, their daughter (not old enough to kill); and Brigitte, the Swiss nanny.

Then there's the crew. Margo, the production manager, turns out to have been one of Alan's lovers. So was Amy, the continuity person. The muscular hot-tempered stuntman, Derek, is Amy's husband. Fernando, aka Fern, the casting director, was also, long ago, one of Alan's lovers. Mitch, the producer who wants to direct, is having an affair with Angie (remember, she was Alan's wife). Lucy used to have a co-starring role, but after a drug arrest she lost it to Annie, the heroine/investigator. Lucy wants her part back. Lazlo is the cinematographer—-he, too, wants to direct.

Alan was last seen alive in public a few minutes after 5:00 P.M. He returned from scouting locations with Amy and Margo. Lazlo stayed behind, to watch the lighting. Alan's still-warm corpse was found at 7:05 P.M.

5:00
Gavin: coming home
Brigitte: coming home
Angie: w/daughter Chelsea in hotel
Mitch: at work in production office
Fern: waiting for Alan
Lucy: waiting for Alan
Alan: on location with Amy, Margo, Lazlo
Derek: following Amy & Alan

5:05
Lucy: chats with Fern
Fern: tells Lucy that Alan is hot for Annie, she should try the producer

5:15
Alan: returns to his room with Amy & Margo
Gavin: lurks outside Alan's door
Derek: follows Alan, sees Gavin, leaves

5:20
Alan: fight with wife Angie
Angie: throws Alan out, puts out his suitcase, calls front desk
Gavin: outside, overhears fight
Fern: to Alan, hears fight, sees Gavin, sees Alan leave, follows him
Mitch: to his own room

5:30
Gavin: goes to Brigitte
Brigitte: tells Gavin she will "take care of it," goes to what is
    now Alan's old room
Angie: goes to Mitch
Mitch: makes love to Angie
Derek: goes to Alan's old room to confront him

5:50
Fern: follows Alan to his new room
Brigitte: goes to new room, overhears Fern fighting with Alan
Derek: discovers Alan has a new room, goes there, hears Fern there
Lazlo: watches the sunset, returns to hotel

Or it might be laid out like this:

Gavin	Brigitte	Margo	Fern	Amy	Derek	Lucy	Angie	Mitch	Lazlo
	goes to Mitch's room to get Angie		leaves Alan's room				dresses, runs out with Brigitte, forgets panties	stuffs panties in drawer	
	goes to Alan's room as he goes out to Annie's room			in room; worries about what Derek will do	about to confront Alan, but Brigitte appears				returns-- must pass, also sees Alan go into Annie's room

The plot will be the process of uncovering all these little bits of information until the whole picture—and the final important clue—is revealed.

If you look at it, you will notice that there are a whole series of points at which one character is in a position to observe—

and inform on—some other character. Gavin hears the fight between his parents. Brigitte tells Gavin she will "take care of things." Derek hears the fight between Fern and Alan and sees Gavin lurking about. Brigitte catches Angie in Mitch's room with her panties off, and so on. Who sees what establishes part of the logic that you, the writer, must follow to make it unfold. In the reality of working, however, the murder is not a fixed event. You made it up. You can change it. In fact, writers work back and forth.

I create similar charts. The first one I make is a generic blank and I print out several copies. Then I can pencil in events and see which goes where and if it will fit. I also make chapter lists with one-line—or one-word—summaries of what happens in each in order to keep track of where I've been and what incident leads to other incidents. Most screenwriting books suggest writing scene descriptions on index cards, which can then be tacked or taped to the wall and moved around, creating a chart with movable parts. You need a largish blank wall space for this method.

If you're the sort of person who likes to learn about things by taking them apart, I think it would be a great exercise to break down your favorite crime novel into an event-by-event outline.

When it comes to sitting down and doing it, everybody goes about it a different way.

Jeff Abbott (*Do Unto Others*, *The Only Good Yankee*, *Promises of Home*, *Distant Blood*, all from Ballantine) does this:

> *I draw my characters and their relationships on an artist's sketch pad. When I'm done, this sketch looks a lot like a spider's web—I know the basic connections each character has with the three most important personalities in the book—the detective, the murderer and his victim. That's*

about all the advance plotting that I do; I don't outline. I keep this sketch near me and add to it as I start writing the first draft. By the end of the book, the sketch doesn't bear an exact resemblance to what I've written, but it always serves to get me started.

William Bernhardt (*Primary Justice, Blind Justice, Deadly Justice, Perfect Justice, Cruel Justice, Double Jeopardy, The Code of Buddyhood*, all published by Ballantine) does this:

I jot ideas down. When it's finally time to start cooking, I sit down with all these notes and try to figure out how they could fit together to make a plot. Inevitably, some of the ideas will not fit, but many of them will, and before long, I begin to see the structure for a possible novel. Then I sit down with a stack of index cards and start organizing it. I use index cards so that, when I finally realize that what I have down as chapter 5 should really be chapter 12, it can be easily moved to the bottom of the stack. What I write on the card is not detailed; it's just enough to give me some structure for my writing.

Personally, I like to know several things before I start. Two of the big ones are the beginning and the end.

The beginning is the situation that gives rise to the rest of the story. Here are three examples.

1. A lawyer, convicted of embezzlement, is threatened with hard time in Attica, and decides to tell all about his client if it will get him off.
2. Two gangsters have a meeting with the son of another in order to have him convince his incarcerated father not to testify against the attorney general of the United States, but it gets out of hand when they kill the gangster's son.

3. Lee Atwater, famous political consultant, comes up with a mad scheme to ensure George Bush's reelection.

The end, the resolution of the story, is your destination. To know it means that you can shape your story. If you don't know where the story is going to end up, it's really hard to decide which roads to travel, what has to be accomplished along the way, and what is completely unnecessary. To put it another way, knowing the end in advance is vastly more economical than not knowing it.

In practice, knowing it and then changing it is just fine. At least it has been for me. It does the requisite job of requiring certain action and keeping me off long, long, long meandering paths from which there is no return.

It is the difference between setting out on a journey you know not where and you know not for what reason and setting out on a journey to Paris to find your ex-spouse. Even if you don't get to Paris, you have a story about how you tried and what made you fail.

Here are two samples and one amusing anecdote.

The amusing anecdote is this: When my first novel was optioned for a movie, there was a clause in it that gave the production company a perpetual option on all sequels if they made the first one into a film. In the event that they did not exercise the option on any subsequent book, I would be free to sell it elsewhere. However, the film company would retain rights to the names of all the characters named in the book they had filmed. These included the hero, his partner, his girlfriend, and her child.

John D. MacDonald wrote over twenty Travis McGee novels. Only one was ever made into a film. It wasn't very successful and it wasn't very good. I suspected that a clause like this was exactly the reason none of the others were produced. The fact that Elmore Leonard does not write series characters is one of the reasons that almost every single one of his books has been made into a film.

Almost simultaneously, my publisher made it clear to me that the only thing for which he would give me an advance based on a proposal would be a series. So I had to choose between income now and possible future earnings.

It was this circumstance that created the ending of *You Get What You Pay For*. I envisioned a scene in which the hero is at a meeting with his lawyer and his accountant. The accountant says, "My advice to you is leave the country." Then the lawyer adds, "And while you're at it, *change your name*."

This was a wonderful ending for me, the story builder, because it says: Build me a story that puts the hero in the position of having to leave the country and change his name. This gave shape to everything. Structurally the book was designed to ultimately and inevitably maneuver him into that situation.

In addition I wanted the events and atmosphere I created along the way to resonate with that ending, to give it added meaning and depth. So it shaped both what would happen and the tone in which it would happen.

In the first two books the attitude was: If this had been a real case, given to a real detective, with this guy's sort of resources in this real world, how could he have possibly gone about doing his job? But my third book, *Foreign Exchange*, was much more *storylike*. I don't have an exact definition of that term, but what it meant to me was that story satisfaction had more to do with determining the internal logic of the book than the considerations of realism of my previous books. Although I did not know who done it, and I changed my mind several times, I did know the ending. I was going to steal, or as we say in literary circles, pay homage to, or if you prefer, run a riff on, one of the most *storylike* and delightful end scenes I've ever seen. It is from the film *The African*

Queen. The river rat, Humphrey Bogart, and the missionary's prim spinster sister, Katharine Hepburn, have traveled down an African river together. It has been an arduous and dangerous journey in the course of which they have fallen in love and, in spite of massive social barriers, clearly slept together. The war in distant Europe has come to the dark continent. A German gunboat dominates the lake at the end of the river. Their goal is to reach the lake and find some way to sink that boat. They turn the *African Queen*, Bogie's ramshackle boat, into a ram with torpedoes in the bow. But a storm comes up. The *Queen* is capsized. They are captured by the Germans, who decide to execute them and to carry out the sentence on the spot, by hanging. As they are about to be hanged, Bogie asks the German captain if he would marry them first: "It would mean so much to the lady." Kate is overwhelmingly touched. This gesture of love and respect and caring is so powerful that they are prepared to die without the least regret. The ceremony takes place. As the ropes are being put around their necks we see the hulk of the overturned *Queen*, homemade torpedoes still intact, drifting into the course of the German gunboat. The gunboat hits the *Queen*. The torpedoes explode and sink the Germans. Bogie and Kate swim off into the sunset.

I love this ending because it is so incredibly contrived and yet it is moving and satisfying and altogether wonderful.

Once again, for me the story builder, this was a great ending because it is so structurally complex. To set it up, a half dozen or so major things had to be placed in position. The hero, heroine, villains, someone to do the marrying, everybody had to end up in the same place at the same time.

The torpedoes (not literal ones, but something that performed the torpedo function) had to be created, then hidden, then launched at the appropriate time.

Working backward, this scene told me a lot about what had to come before.

The fact that it was so contrived was part of its appeal. It meant that all the things that led up to it had to be well constructed and suspension of disbelief had to be maintained, in order to get away with it. Each character needed good, reasonable, and compelling reasons for being in that room, at that exact time, and for reacting as each one did. The primary male-female relationship had to be designed so that the marriage becomes a moment of great sentiment, as well as a plot device. If the motivations were not up to snuff, the structure would become nakedly visible, offensively visible, as some forms of nudity are.

An ending is a great tool for organizing a story.

The next thing I want to have before I start is a bunch of high points. High points function like mini endings. They, too, are things that you must build toward.

High points may be emotional scenes. One of the most extraordinary and affecting scenes I've ever read comes from Thomas Harris's *Red Dragon*. It's a flashback to the birth of the serial killer.

The obstetrician remarked that he looked "more like a leaf-nosed bat than a baby," another truth. He was born with bilateral fissures in his upper lip and in his hard and soft palates. The center section of his mouth was unanchored and protruded. His nose was flat.

The hospital supervisors decided not to show him to his mother immediately. They waited to see if the infant could survive without oxygen. They put him in a bed at the rear of the infant ward and faced him away from the viewing window. He could breathe, but he could not feed. With his palate cleft, he could not suck.

His mother abandons him. A surgeon makes some repairs; "the cosmetic results were not good." The child is sent to an orphanage. Brother Buddy, the head of the orphanage, "called the other boys and girls together and told them that Francis was a harelip but they must be careful never to call him a harelip."

> *Near the end of this fifth year, Francis Dolarhyde had his first and only visitor at the orphanage.*
>
> *. . . What struck Francis, what he would always remember: she smiled with pleasure when she saw his face. That had never happened before. No one would ever do it again.*
>
> *"This is your grandmother," Brother Buddy said.*
>
> *"Hello," she said.*
>
> *Brother Buddy wiped his mouth with a long hand. "Say 'hello.' Go ahead."*
>
> *Francis had learned to say some things by occluding his nostrils with his upper lip, but he did not have much occasion for "hello." "Lhho" was the best he could do.*
>
> *Grandmother seemed even more pleased with him. "Can you say 'grandmother'?"*
>
> *"Try to say 'grandmother,' " Brother Buddy said.*
>
> *The plosive G defeated him. Francis strangled easily on tears.*
>
> *. . . "Never mind," his grandmother said. "I'll just bet he can say his name. I just know a big boy like you can say his name. Say it for me."*
>
> *The child's face brightened. The big boys had helped him with this. He wanted to please. He collected himself.*
>
> *"Cunt Face," he said.*

It's so cruel and hurtful that it transforms the villain—who is incredibly horrific—into a sympathetic creature. There's lots of blood and gore, yet this is, for me, the most memorable scene in the book.

One of my major literary influences was *Mad Magazine*'s "Scenes We'd Like to See." These were heavy-handed reverses of movie clichés. Possibly the most famous is the one with the Lone Ranger and Tonto surrounded by angry Indians. The Lone Ranger prepares for battle, and says something like "Looks like we're in heap big trouble now, kimosabe." Tonto looks at him and says, "What do you mean *we*, pale face?" I look to do scenes like that: build toward the cliché and undercut it with a swift application of reality.

I've always had a thing about Spenser's sidekick, Hawk, in the series by Robert Parker. Hawk's the baddest of bad African-American persons. He has a Marvin Hagler head shave and owns lots of expensive consumer items. I've always felt that this is a cheap racist contrivance—the Bwana Seal of Approval. Hero so good that even the darky jungle savage who don' like no white man like him. Parker is hardly the only person to use this device. It's hugely popular. I'm guilty of it too. Any third world person will do. Andrew Vachss uses a Mongolian. It crops up in James Bond and Indiana Jones films, among others. So, as one of the set pieces in *American Hero*, I decided to have a scene in which someone says: "Never trust no nigger calls himself Hawk and dresses like a pimp." As a matter of political correctness I could only have an African-American person say this. This set piece—just one sentence actually—dictated the creation of two characters: one to say it and one to say it about. It required a scene in which it was said. That scene required a series of events that preceded it in order to set it up. And if I was going to be a good craftsman about it, I had to do all of that sufficiently well so that it was effective on its own terms and worked even if the reader had never heard of Parker, Spenser, or Hawk.

I am sure there are people who like whole, detailed outlines. I don't. Either because I am too lazy for that much clear thought or because for me there is too much interplay between all the factors. Scenes, which have their own inner logic, and get their rhythm as they are written, frequently go further or stop shorter than I had planned or would like. That, in turn, suggests and often requires a change in what follows. Characters, emotional effects, things that I thought would work but don't, and the things that I substitute all require constant plot adjustment.

There are writers who claim they don't know where they intend to go. They start with characters and a situation and just bull their way forward. That's interesting. In the first draft of this book there was a sentence that says: "And having mentioned it, I shall probably try it sometime." As I wrote the second draft I was doing it.

It is, as I suspected then, uneconomical. Also difficult. Also somewhat frightening in that it can lead to starting books that cannot be finished.

The full outline, or even the demi-guide of knowing the opening, the final resolve, a couple of peaks, and some of the passes through the mountains, gives you a glimpse of the final realization, an idea, not just of how you might finish the book, but of whether the work can be satisfactorily completed.

In creating the book, the opening gives you the springboard from which you launch the story.

The end is an anchor point that allows you to shape and structure the middle.

I experience the middle as rather like a chess game. Each time I create an event I imagine it through to the end game almost exactly the way a chess player thinks through the possible consequence of each move. Sometimes I have to consider a lot of different moves before I can visualize a sequence that will take me through to a satisfactory endgame.

A COUPLE OF USEFUL DEVICES

1. A cast list. Every time I put a character down on the page, I put him on the cast list. I use the cut-and-paste feature on my program to include his first description, and some-times later descriptions.

2. A trim bin. That's a film editor's term. When you're cut-ting film and you cut off little bits and pieces that are shorter than scenes, you hang them from their sprocket holes on a rack fixed above a bin. The bin is there be-cause pieces of film might be yards long and you don't want them dragging on the floor (which is irrelevant to our topic), but whenever I trim a bit that might be re-motely useful, I cut and paste it into a file that I call by that name.

3. Keep an ongoing outline of what you've written.

CHAPTER 3

Openings

Opening scenes should be strong and—like a lead paragraph in a news story—summarize the entire book. Every book and article on writing emphasizes the importance of your first page. Basically they say that if you don't grab the readers with the first page, first paragraph, first sentence, they will stop reading. And they will.

Watch bookstore shoppers. If placement or the author's reputation or the jacket induces them to open a book, what do they look at? Page one. Maybe something at random around the middle. Some people look at the end, but they are despicable and they probably won't buy the book anyway.

Professional readers—publishers, contest judges, reviewers selecting which book to review—who can't read all of every book will read page one. If they are thorough sorts of people, they'll read chapter one plus a middle chapter plus the end chapter.

If you, as a writer, are in the pleasant position of being able to get an advance based on a proposal, that proposal will be the first fifty to seventy-five pages and an outline of the rest. The purpose of the outline is to prove that there is some way that a book based on the premise of the opening can be finished. It is not, in practice, a promise that you will finish it exactly that way. If you find a successful way to complete the book and anyone even remembers what you wrote in the outline, the most they're likely to say is, "Umm, interesting, found a different way to work out the story, umm." I'd better advise you that if you run into an editor who doesn't feel that way, who thinks you should have followed the outline, and who regards the proposal as tantamount to contract specifications, it will do you no good at all to cite this essay.

The peculiar thing is that all these people who look to the openings *are right to do so.* I have about six shelves of mysteries. The top one is books that I truly respect, the stuff that I think is the best in the field, that I am not ashamed to be seen reading, that I would be proud to be compared to, that I steal from. When I was examining openings for a friend of mine, I pulled down several, more or less at random. I discovered to our mutual interest and edification that each of these books nails it right out of the gate:

The Crazy Kill: Chester Himes

It was four o'clock, Wednesday morning, July 14th, in Harlem, U.S.A. Seventh Avenue was as dark and lonely as haunted graves.

A colored man was stealing a bag of money.

The Spy Who Came In from the Cold: John Le Carré
[the middle of page one]

"He's waiting for the dark," Leamas muttered, "I know he is."

"This morning you said he'd come across with the workmen."

Leamas turned on him. "Agents aren't airplanes. They don't have schedules. He's blown, he's on the run, he's frightened. Mundt's after him, now, at this moment. He's got only one chance. Let him choose the time."

Gorky Park: Martin Cruz Smith [paragraph three]

The investigator suspected the poor dead bastards were just a vodka troika that had cheerily frozen to death. Vodka was liquid taxation, and the price was always rising. It was accepted that three was the lucky number on a bottle in terms of economic prudence and desired effect. It was a perfect example of primitive communism.

Red Harvest: Dashiell Hammett

I first heard Personville called Poisonville by a red-haired mucker named Hickey Dewey in the Big Ship in Butte. He also called shirt a shoit. I didn't think anything of what he had done to the city's name. Later I heard men who could manage their r's give it the same pronunciation. I still didn't see anything in it but the meaningless sort of humor that used to make richardsnary the thieves' word for dictionary. A few years later I went to Personville and learned better.

Darker Than Amber: John D. MacDonald

*We were about to give up and call it a night when some-
body dropped the girl off the bridge.*

Kennedy for the Defense: George V. Higgins

*I have a client named Teddy Franklin. Teddy Franklin is a
car thief. He is 32 years old and is one of the best car
thieves on the Eastern Seaboard. Cadillac Ted is so good
he is able to support himself as a car thief. He has been
arrested repeatedly, but he has never done time. That is
because I am good. It is also because Teddy is so good.
    Teddy is as cute as a shithouse rat. . . .*

Note that these do not merely grab you—each one of
them is the whole book in one scene. Actually in just a
few lines. Or even in just one sentence. I was impressed. And
still am.

If I were to run a contest for best first sentence that contains the whole book, it would be:

The Godfather: Mario Puzo

*Amerigo Bonasera sat in New York Criminal Court Num-
ber 3 and waited for justice; vengeance on the men who
had so cruelly hurt his daughter, who had tried to dis-
honor her.*

I was curious to see if cozies, which I rarely read, worked
the same way. The only one I found on the shelf was *Sad
Cypress,* by Agatha Christie. It begins this way:

"Elinor Katherine Carlisle. You stand charged upon this indictment with the murder of Mary Gerrard upon the 27th of July last. Are you guilty or not guilty?"

. . . Sir Edwin Bulmer, counsel for the Defense, felt a thrill of dismay. He thought, My God, she's going to plead guilty. She's lost her nerve.

Right on, Agatha!

I mentioned this to my agent. "Everybody does great openings nowadays," she said. With a certain annoyance.

"Yeah," her husband said. He worked for her at that time and read a lot of the manuscripts. "It's as if they all went to the same writing school and took a class in openings."

There was my great discovery shot down. Nonetheless, I continued to think about it. The exciting opening is not, at its best, just a gimmick or a literary affectation. *It is a scene that unleashes forces.* You know that from such an event, this story has got to go places. It's going to take off. It has narrative drive. Because that's another way to look at what narrative drive is: force or forces that push the story forward.

John Grisham has great openings.

A Time to Kill begins with a brutal rape scene in a rural section of Mississippi. Two crude, nasty, low-class white men assault and almost kill a young and innocent African-American girl. She manages to survive and to escape. Her father finds out what happened and he goes and kills them. This is, as we all know, a culture that frowns upon black men killing white men. A place in which just a few years ago an African-American might be killed for drinking water at a whites-only water fountain, or attempting to vote. But it is also a place and a society that expects a good father to do exactly what this father did. A father who did less would be something less than a man.

The bulk of the book is the trial of the father. Everybody concerned will have deep, passionate feelings about the case.

Grisham's most recent book, *The Rainmaker*, begins:

My decision to become a lawyer was irrevocably sealed when I realized my father hated the legal profession. I was a young teenager . . . about to be shipped off to a military school by my father for insubordination. He was an ex-Marine who believed boys should live by the crack of the whip. I'd developed . . . an aversion to discipline and his solution was simply to send me away. It was years before I forgave him.

He was also an industrial engineer who worked seventy hours a week for a company that made, among many other items, ladders. Because by their very nature ladders are dangerous devices, his company became a frequent target of lawsuits. And because he handled design, my father was the favorite choice to speak for the company in depositions and trials. I can't say that I blame him for hating lawyers, but I grew to admire them because they made his life so miserable.

. . . The day after I learned I had been accepted to law school, I proudly returned home with this great news. Mother told me later he stayed in bed for a week.

Two weeks after my triumphant visit, he was changing a lightbulb in the utility room when (I swear this is true) a ladder collapsed and he fell on his head.

The hero is a young man who needs, desperately, to prove himself. Grisham will combine that with an opponent who is a clear and vigorous father figure and a victim who dies because an insurance company refused his legitimate claim. Another example:

> *The decision to bomb the office of the radical Jew lawyer was reached with relative ease. Only three people were involved in the process. The first was the man with the money. The second was a local operative who knew the territory. And the third was a young patriot and zealot with a talent for explosives and an astonishing knack for disappearing without a trail. After the bombing, he fled the country and hid in northern Ireland.*
>
> John Grisham, *The Chamber*

The bombing, detailed in the next ten pages, is particularly gruesome and horrific. It doesn't kill the lawyer, but it does require both of his legs to be amputated below the knee. It kills his two young children, who were visiting him at the office. One of the bombers is convicted and sentenced to death. The hero is a slick young Chicago lawyer who's going to handle the death row appeal. He's also the bomber's grandson.

Grisham has a knack for finding or creating situations that will bring powerful and primal emotions into play.

A great beginning unleashes the forces that will propel the rest of the book.

CHAPTER 4

Scene Construction

The opening of a scene (section or chapter or segment) establishes a problem. A problem is a situation for which someone is seeking a solution. It may be a situation for which several people are seeking several different solutions. That desire creates forward motion, known in this book as narrative drive.

The bulk of the scene, the middle, is the effort to resolve, to overcome, the obstacles and solve the problem.

The end of the scene is the resolution of the problem. Though it may not be, probably should not be, the resolution sought at the beginning.

Scene construction is, in miniature, book construction.

The difference between the construction of the book and the construction of the scene is that the setup for most chapters, after the first one or two, takes place in previous chapters and that the resolve is not just an end, it is also a launching pad for a new problem.

This is what it looks like.

Here's how it works.

The Maltese Falcon, Chapter One, entitled "Spade and Archer": Sam Spade is in his office. His secretary comes in and says they have a new client and that Sam will want to see her, "she's a knockout." Miss Wonderly enters. She says she has a missing little sister, she wants a PI to locate her by following the guy she ran away with, Floyd Thursby. In mid-scene Sam's partner, Miles Archer, comes in. He's also attracted to Miss Wonderly. At the end of the scene he promises the new client that he will take care of it personally. When she's gone he says, "Maybe you saw her first, Sam, but I spoke first."

The initial direction of the scene is, Sam gets a new client. Miles gets in the way. The new direction is that it's Archer's case.

Chapter Two, "Death in the Fog": Miles has been shot while on that job. That's the new problem. It was set up by the resolve of the previous scene.

Spade goes to the scene of the crime. He calls his secretary and has her call his partner's wife, the new widow. He walks the streets. Goes home.

The logical suspect is Thursby, and Sam will probably go off and try to find him. Then cops come and question Sam. They reveal that Thursby has been shot too. There's that brick wall. A dead end. Have to go somewhere new.

Chapter Three, "Three Women": Once again the new scene starts with a twist on the direction provided by the old scene. Eva, Miles's widow, shows up, dressed in black. She throws her arms around Sam, kisses him, and asks him if he killed Miles.

Then we find out that Eva wasn't home at the time of the murder. A new direction. At least a possibility.

Miss Wonderly has checked out of her hotel, no forwarding address. Another new direction.

Then she calls. New address, new name.

Chapter Four, "The Black Bird": The bulk of the scene is the development of a new relationship between the ever more complex Miss Wonderly, aka LeBlanc, aka Brigid O'Shaughnessy, and Spade. They're going to work together. Then Joel Cairo walks in.

He's the first to mention the black bird. A whole new spin on things. Even within this snippet, a two-page scene at the end of the chapter, we have forward motion: Cairo tries to hire Spade, Spade seems to agree, then—with a complete change of direction—Cairo pulls a gun on Sam.

As a matter of working process, what I like to know about a chapter before I write it is what I like to know about a book: the opening, the close, and a couple of high points.

Knowing the end of the scene helps you avoid being boring. You are boring when the reader knows what will happen next. You are not boring when the reader is surprised. That would seem to imply that the resolution, the end scene, must be new and original.

This may or may not be an answer. Yes, new and original will help eliminate boredom. But remember that readers and, frequently even more so, editors want SOS (same old stuff), especially in the resolution: the story builds, with ever-increasing danger, to a climax in which the hero confronts the villian, the good guy wins, the crime is solved, and the hero gets the girl and the gold watch.

Upon a second look we realize that the structure has three parts, and we can beat the bored "I know exactly where this is going" feeling in any one of the three, but most especially in the middle.

The technique is the same as a magic trick, the essence is *misdirection*. We state the problem. That's part one. Then we look for the solution resolutely facing away from the resolve that we are actually going to use. We write the bulk of the scene going in the direction of the false resolution. It must be a logical, reasonably likely resolution. This requires a certain amount of balance and craft(iness) because the real resolve must also be prepared so that it doesn't appear arbitrary, but not so overprepared that you telegraph it. That's what makes a twist feel like a twist.

It's a lot like telling a joke—there's the setup and the punch line. Look at joke construction. The setup, for the most part, is a case of misdirection. Setting up one expectation, then paying off from another direction.

Like this one, which purports to explain Jewish logic. It is supposed to be told with Yiddish accents. Imagine them if you like.

"Vaiter," the customer calls. "Taste the soup."
The waiter says, "Whattsamatta with the soup?"
"Taaaste the soup."
"It's too hot? Too cold?"
"Vaiter, taste the soup."
"If you don't like the soup, say so. . . ."
"Vaiter, taste the soup."
"You vant another bowl of soup?"
"Vaiter, taste the soup."
"We got lots other kinds of soup. We got pea soup, matzo ball, chicken . . ."
"Vaiter, taste the soup."
"All right already. Vhere's the spoon?"
"Ahhh-hah!"

Scene construction is not an academic theory. It is a cold-blooded manipulation of your audience. It's one of the primary tricks for making them turn the page.

Every scene starts with THE PROBLEM, then appears to drive toward RESOLUTION A but always gets thrown to RESOLUTION B. Every RESOLVE creates a new PROBLEM. Each scene has a hook at the end.

What's a hook? Where can I get one? Can I make my own?

CHAPTER 5

Hooks & Tales

A hook is an ending that raises a new question—or new problem—even more urgent than the one we solved. *The Godfather*, one of the most perfectly constructed crime novels ever written, hooks relentlessly. So much so that the last sentence of each chapter is almost always exactly that, an explicit hook.

Chapter One in the book, just as in the movie, is the famous wedding scene. This scene gathers virtually all the important players in the story and establishes who they are.

Part of the mythology of Godfather weddings, at least according to Mario Puzo, is that on such a day the Godfather can deny no one's request. As a result there is a whole line of people waiting to see him with urgent problems. Every single one of these is a story line that needs resolution. It includes a thinly disguised Frank Sinatra character, an undertaker whose daughter has been beaten up, subgangsters who want more power, and a dying consigliere. The consigliere knows he's about to go to hell, so he wants the Godfather to put in the fix with God.

It also introduces Don Corleone's three sons. Santino, "Sonny," the oldest, is a gangster with a violent temper. The middle son is a weakling. The youngest, Michael, is the best and brightest, a decorated veteran of the just-ended Second World War, a student at an Ivy League college. He is slated to assimilate and to go legitimate. Tom Hagen is an unofficially adopted fourth son who has been raised with the boys. He's a lawyer.

The Godfather has been stalling negotiations with a criminal named Sollozzo until after the wedding because he knows that these matters will end in a gang war.

In Chapter Two the war begins.

Don Corleone is shot down in the street. His sons and the other leaders in his gang gather and prepare for war. Luca Brazi has been established in the previous chapter as one of the pillars of the Godfather's power, a killer, the family's number one enforcer. The last line of the chapter is: "With Luca Brazi and the resources of the Corleone Family there could be but one outcome. But again the nagging worry. Where was Luca Brazi?"

Chapter Three: Tom Hagen, now the new consigliere, is kidnapped by Sollozzo, who promises that he means Hagen no harm, that his intent is to use Hagen to convince the hotheaded Santino Corleone to make a deal rather than go to war. The phone rings. Sollozzo listens, then says to Hagen: " 'The old man is still alive. Five bullets in his Sicilian hide and he's still alive.' He gave a fatalistic shrug. 'Bad luck,' he said to Hagen. 'Bad luck for me. Bad luck for you.' "

Chapter Four: Hotheaded Sonny is in charge. He announces that the family will go to war, that he will personally kill Sollozzo. He plans to use Luca Brazi to kill the

Tattaglias, another crime family, who backed Sollozzo. Sonny reveals that he "made his bones" (killed his first man) when he was nineteen, the last time the family went to war. Michael is to be kept out of the war, out of the gangster side of the family business. That's the Godfather's plan. It is also Michael's plan. Tom Hagen, released by Sollozzo, arrives.

> He [Hagen] hadn't lived with the Corleone Family ten years for nothing, Michael thought with a queer flush of pride. Some of the old man had rubbed off on him, as it had on Sonny, and he thought, with surprise, even on himself.

Chapter Five: Michael insists on doing something. OK, Sonny says, you can be on the telephone.

> Michael didn't say anything. He felt awkward, almost ashamed, and he noticed Clemenza and Tessio [the two underbosses] with faces so carefully impassive that he was sure that they were hiding their contempt. He picked up the phone and dialed Luca Brazi's number and kept the receiver to his ear as it rang and rang.

And so on. I will include one more, because I love it so, and because it launches not just another scene, but a whole back story. Michael goes to the hospital to visit his father. His father is supposed to be under guard, both by his own people and by the police. But no one is there. Michael realizes an assassination is planned. He moves his father to another room.

> Michael leaned over the bed. He took his father's hand in his. "It's Mike," he said. "Don't be afraid. Now listen,

don't make any noise at all, especially if somebody calls out your name. Some people want to kill you, understand? But I'm here so don't be afraid."

Don Corleone, still not fully conscious of what had happened to him the day before, in terrible pain, yet smiling benevolently on his youngest son, wanted to tell him, but it was too much effort, "Why should I be afraid now? Strange men have come to kill me ever since I was twelve years old."

CHAPTER 6

Clarity

Clarity is the essence of all good writing. Of any type. It is the absolute basic, from the phrase to the sentence to the book. If I were ever to teach writing or composition or rhetoric or grammar or creative writing, I would teach one thing and it would be the same thing to all—clarity.

The sentence should be, above all, clear.

The rules of grammar are, for the most part, rules of clarity. If you are clear, your grammar, however casual and slanguaged, with whatever personal tics and eccentricities you bring to it, is good grammar. If you have followed all the textbook rules of grammar but you are misunderstood or un-understood, that's bad grammar. Odd punctuation? Fragments of sentences? Nouvelle vocab and undictionaried words? All A-OK. If totally, and easily, comprehensible. If everyone who reads what you have written understands it correctly, it has been written correctly. If every person who reads it understands it easily and fully, it is written well.

There is a "literary" attitude that difficult to read—abstruse matters suffused with elusive and insidious similes, prolix, convoluted, impregnated through misadventure with meretricious metaphor, subtly recondite, parenthetically equivocated with qualifying clauses, redolent of redundancy or, conversely, flat with uninflected minimalism in the spirit of the mannered modernists, appearing to say nothing but actually suggesting an apocryphal intuition of even less—is good.

This perverse attitude is a product of academia. The first and most essential job of a critic is to make himself more important than the work itself, to establish that the work cannot be understood except through the critic's explanation.

This is compounded by the demands of academic institutions. University teachers are expected to do more than merely teach. They are supposed to do research and to publish their results. That is one thing in the sciences and even the social sciences. But it's weird when they have to write papers about the work of other people whose primary purpose was to make themselves understood in the first place. It gets weirder still when there are thousands of them out there writing yet another interpretation of Dickens and Shakespeare. You can see how grateful they would be to find material that is sufficiently incomprehensible that it actually does require explanation. It's an immense relief. And how resentful they might be of work that anyone can pick up and read all by himself.

It is also said that readers want to think, that they want to participate by working at the material, and that part of the job of the writer is to make the reader think. There is some truth in that. But think about what?

It may be reasonable to ask readers to meditate deeply on

the burning issues of the day or on eternal issues of God and Death, War and Peace, Eros and Ethics, but it's not sensible to ask them to memorize the names of your fictional population and remember that Jody is the male DA and Blake is the six-foot-one-inch female hit person and Cody is the African-American hermaphrodite and Drake is the pornographer who photographed Cody and Jody licking the secretions of psychedelic toads that had been raised by Judy and Chris.

Should the reader have to stop and count lines of dialogue backward to figure out who is speaking when a simple "John said" or "Sheila said" would tell him?

When someone named Fred walks into the room in Chapter Twenty-six, should the reader have to leaf his way back through the book all the way to Chapter—what chapter was it? Nine? Twelve? Oh God, this is annoying! Four? Yes! No. I can't find it. Damn it. (Throw the book against the wall. Pick it up.) Ah, there it is! Seven, the only previous time Fred appeared, to find out that he is the psychotic brother of the heroine, that he's the six-foot-two-inch bearded, bald man who always carries a Khyber knife.

These things should be as simple and clear as "See Spot Run."

My own academic background, such as it is, and heretofore rarely admitted to in public, is in theater. One of the interesting things about theater history is that *all* the Great Plays were written in periods when the theater was vastly popular, popular across all class lines. All other theater is trivial and narrow and, with the passage of time, of interest only to the academician. All the great plays are clear and, at least on their surface, absolutely transparent and easy to understand.

Even William Shakespeare.

If seen in performance, especially a good one, he's easy to follow and great fun as well. After all, the stuff was written to be played with shouts and swords, flashing eyes and broad gestures, not to be read in high school English classes. I just saw *Taming of the Shrew* in Prague. It was performed in Czech, one of the many languages I don't speak. I understood the performance perfectly. At one time I worked for the New York Shakespeare Festival Mobile Theater, which produced Shakespeare's plays for free in the neighborhoods of New York. Every sort of audience, of every class and ethnic group, understood *Henry V* and *Macbeth* and was visibly responsive to them.

Art—unlike criticism or lecturing—is actually a dialogue, not a monologue. The writer, or any other kind of artist, is in a conversation with society or a segment thereof. The narrower the segment, the narrower the vision and the more constricted the conversation. During the Golden Age of Greece the entire city went to the theater, all at once. Aeschylus, Sophocles, and Euripides had to impress the likes of Socrates and Plato and at the same time keep the buffoons and mule drivers awake.

You will find thrillers on the shelves of truck drivers and presidents. Kennedy loved James Bond, Ronald Reagan's endorsement of Tom Clancy made him a bestseller, and Bill Clinton has been photographed shopping at mystery bookstores.

Clarity is the door that lets the whole world in.

From the clarity of the sentence we go to the clarity of the paragraph or group of paragraphs. We go from making each discrete bit of thought clear to organizing a series of thoughts in a way that is clear and easy to understand.

First and most simply, there is the issue of order. Some thoughts must precede others. Some must follow.

The writer has to make a choice of what must be explained and what need not be explained. Remember, you are having a dialogue. Imagine the faces of the group around you listening. You can lose them by telling them what they already know. You can lose them by failing to provide essential parts of the story.

How can you tell?

One trick is to read your work out loud. It will make a lot of things obvious. Also, if you get bored listening to yourself, they will, too. If you don't think it's clear, they will find it even less clear.

Your own judgment is not perfect. Nor is mine. That's a universal truth. It is in the nature of things that sometimes you will be wrong. Some things that you think are clear are not clear. What do you do about that?

Let other people read your work. If they don't understand something, that means that it's not clear.

Your initial reaction will probably be that they must be really dumb not to understand what you have written with such clarity. That might be true. But it is irrelevent. You are not writing it so that you can understand it. You are writing it so they can understand it. That's your job. So change it. And thank them for letting you know.

Sometimes clarity clashes, or appears to clash, with style. That is an illusion and an indulgence. Clarity is God and must be served first.

If you wish to serve style as well, you may do so, but it must come after clarity and be subservient to it.

Dick Francis is a terrific example to study for clarity. And conciseness as well. He's always explaining how things work—finances, horses, toys, horse racing, banking, horse raising, photography, horse breeding, shooting, horse transporting, physical therapy, horse trading. It's always simple and clear.

They were thirty-five-millimeter color film negatives, and there were a lot of them, some simply blank and others blank with uneven magenta blotches here and there. . . .

While slide film—transparencies—appears to the eye in their true lifelike colors, negative film appeared in the reciprocal colors: and to get back to the true colors one had of course to make a print from the negative.

The primary colors of light were blue, green, and red. The reciprocal colors, in which they appeared on a negative, were yellow, magenta, and cyan. Negatives therefore would have looked like mixtures of yellow, deep pink (magenta) and greeny-blue (cyan), except that to get good whites and highlights all manufacturers gave their negatives an overall pale orange cast. Color negatives therefore always looked a pale clear orange at the edges.

Dick Francis, *Reflex*

Notice the way the trade word "transparencies" is defined even before it's used. "Reciprocal colors" are explained almost immediately after the expression appears, and he tells us what magenta and cyan are because we don't really know. Would that our school texts had been so clear on subjects no more difficult and complex. Had they been so, we all would have been A students and even enjoyed the process of what they called learning.

It is important to note that Francis's explanations are fascinating and powerful because they are intrinsic to the action. The mechanics of the business or trade explained are also the mechanics whereby the crime is committed and whereby the crime is solved.

The preceding passage continues thusly:

The overall orange color also had the effect of masking the yellow sections so that they didn't show to the eye as yellow bits of negative but as orange.

> *[These] negatives looked a pale clear transparent orange throughout.*
>
> *Just suppose, I thought, that under the orange there was an image in yellow which at the moment didn't show.*
>
> *If I printed those negatives the yellow would become blue.*
>
> *An invisible yellow negative image could turn into a totally visible printed image in blue.*

To separate the issues of clarity from the other techniques of fiction, I think it's worthwhile to read nonfiction. A rather incomplete and very random list created by turning around and looking at my shelves would include anything by Tom Wolfe, (the new) Adam Smith, Robert Caro, Robert Daly, Isaac Asimov, Abbie Hoffman, or, by title: *The Band Played On, Fatal Subtraction, Innocents at Home, The Fatal Shore, Serpico, The Blooding.*

Likewise, writing nonfiction is great practice for writing clear fiction. Writing nonfiction that is easy and clear, that is dramatic and entertaining, is even better practice.

The issue of clarity is not limited to explaining the Federal Reserve System concisely and coherently so that we understand how some brilliant heist can be engineered. It's just a bit simpler to notice clarity in informational material. It's quite vital for all the rest.

Clarity is the essence of writing action scenes. The reader needs to understand—effortlessly, without drawing charts, sketching the room on a notepad, or checking back three pages—where everyone is, how they're armed or unarmed, whose side they're on, what they want to accomplish, and how the opposing forces compare to each other. Every move each person makes and its implications should be instantly understood. Except, of course, when you are holding something back for surprise.

Clarity is the essence of communicating character and motivation. You must be clear in your own mind who people are and why they do things; otherwise you can't make them credible or consistent.

You must be clear even in your ambiguities, deceptions, and lies.

CHAPTER 7

Sex

THE HOW-TO

A good sex scene, like any other good scene, is a matter of construction. Problem, movement toward a solution (setup), a surprise solution (payoff). If it's not the end of the book, it should create a new problem that will require a new solution (the hook).

A husband and wife go away to an isolated cabin in the woods. They decide to play some happy erotic games. He handcuffs her to the bed. She changes her mind, kicks him to prove she means it. He has a heart attack and dies. She's alone. Handcuffed. This is *Gerald's Game*, by Stephen King, and it launches a whole new set of actions, both forward and backward in time, and the scene resonates with much of what else the book is about.

A detective has seen nude photographs of a very beautiful woman in the company of a man he is trying to investigate.

After much effort, he locates her. For a variety of good and compelling reasons the detective is trying to remain true and faithful to his spousal equivalent. But there is one of those hot eye-contact connections between the two of them. She invites him back to her apartment. She puts on music, they dance.

Then two Bulgarian weight lifters burst in, pick him up, and throw him out the window. He lands on a lawyer.

This spins the story into new directions.

Sex scenes often don't take place in one compact sequence. They are often built up through many preceding scenes.

Eric Wright gave me this wonderful bit of advice. Eric's books are very, very clean indeed, free of foul words and gynecological detail. They're Canadian. However, the way Eric creates a sex scene is by writing an XXX hard-core version first, with all the explicit bits, where all the parts go, and who says what to whom before, during, and after. Then he goes back and rewrites it, removing anything that might offend his mother or mine or yours.

He now has a clean version that retains some specificity and authenticity.

THE SOCIOLOGY

Sex in crime novels, as in life, exists much less than you think. This is the passage from *Foreign Exchange* that my editor objected to:

> The truth is that I love Marie pregnant. Sexually. This is
> a surprise. All that roundness. I love to take her from be-
> hind and feel the fullness of her buttocks, that waddling
> wideness against my thighs, and my hand weighing the

swollen tits and feeling the shape of her baby-holding belly. She's vibrant, and healthy, and womanly. There's no cancer-scary pills to think about, no age-of-AIDS rubbers, no Catholic rhythmic counting of days, no pulling out just in time. There is a free and mindless ejaculation, thoroughly primitive, into a completely technology-free vaginal canal.

Mild enough, I would have thought. Still, I showed it to a baby group, nursing mothers all, and got their approval before I insisted on keeping it.

My editor had wanted it rewritten to be less specific and "more romantic." I took a look at another book he had edited to try to figure out what he liked and came across this passage from the love scene: "Her nipples were as hard and smooth as pebbles on a beach." (This was not the clue that revealed to the hero that he was making love to an alien, it was meant as an index of erotic excitement.)

However, to the degree that he was expressing a marketing judgment, rather than his taste, there is something in his response that should be considered.

The image of crime novels as sexual—the hard-boiled ones at any rate—comes from an earlier era when people in books "did it" and did it in a variety of enthusiastic ways that appealed to the prurient interest while people on television and in movies and in songs didn't do it. Never, ever.

Nowadays, dancers in rock videos bump and grind in costumes skimpier than what would have had them arrested in Minneapolis back in 1957. T & A is now a staple of prime-time programming. Every cable system has an erotic channel. Prince has a recording called *Come*, a concept album about bringing a woman to an orgasm. It takes the full length of both sides of the album for her to get there. The image of love in Gangsta Rap lyrics is expressed in inches. Advertisements glitter with naked male torsos, sock-stuffed crotches, female cleavage, and buttock cheeks.

Every sexual act, including some never conceived of before technology made them possible, and every sexual relationship—same sex, multiple, intrafamily, solo, video, pain filled, financially based, power skewed, religously affiliated, racially flavored, equipment motivated—has been represented by a spokesperson on a talk show.

Perhaps it is in search of respite that novels have grown less and less sexual. You may immediately think of exceptions, but the current best-selling, genre-transcending novelists—Grisham, Parker, Francis, Le Carré, Ludlum, Paretsky, Grafton—produce work that is remarkably asexual. When I was at a meeting of the International Association of Crime Writers, with twenty or thirty of us there, I asked around, looking for examples for this chapter, if anyone could think of good sex scenes in crime novels.

The response was shocking! No one could think of any.

What sex there is, for the most part, is of two kinds, the perfect and the perverse.

The perfect is what the hero and heroine have. It has nipples "hard as pebbles on a beach," is usually better than ever before, "never had she felt such exquisite pleasure." The curtain is quite frequently drawn over the physiological details. Though it may have some good clean oral and/or digital foreplay, it will certainly end, explicitly or implicitly, as "[she] cried out again, tossing her head, never having felt such intense pleasure in her life. Just at that moment he plunged deep inside her and his body froze like a statue"—or That is to say, with mutual orgasm during genital intercourse. Masters and Johnson told us long ago that this last item is the unlikeliest of events, a physiological improbability.

This is, in my opinion, a shame. Sex is not only a remarkably interesting subject, it is still amazingly shrouded in mythology and lies. The truth is a world full of premature ejaculators, women who can only have orgasm in a particular position and only with one brand of vibrator, people who have never had sex sober, and:

> *It was six inches long. He stroked it lightly, but he could not conjure an appropriate response: eroticism, revulsion, fascination, terror. He had read it described in a hundred melodramatic and pathetic suicide notes. Technology had even infiltrated death messages: So far this year four farewells were transmitted on taped cassettes, the ultimate proof of declining literacy.*
>
> *It was dark and cool in the tiny kitchen. The Formica tabletop was greasy and wet from the spillage of Tullamore Dew. He stroked the thing again. It had hung on his body for too long. More of a cock than the other one. He used it once a month as required by the Los Angeles Police Department. He tried to use the other one this very night. The fifth of Tullamore Dew was nearly empty. He should be anesthetized. He'd nearly died and all he could think of was his cock. But the memory of the misfire hurt.*

That's the first two paragraphs of *The Glitter Dome*, by Joseph Wambaugh, a book that also has a flasher named Tuna Can Tommy, whose name refers to a penis that's only two inches long but three inches wide. Chapter One goes on to explore the misfire referred to above in its psycho-physiologic-alcoholic details. Later in the book there is another funny-sad misfire in a massage parlor. What's wonderful about it is that it's a glimpse of reality and that Wambaugh dares to let it happen to his *hero*.

Real sex, or even partially real sex, is a lot more interesting than fake sex. I wonder, frequently, if the writers of most books I read have ever actually had sex. With penis and vagina—or two of one and none of the other—with real people attached to those parts with all the varied, slightly weird, and very individualistic relations to those parts that real-world people have.

I have been especially disappointed in the lack of sex in books by women with women as heroines. Female sexuality, although it is a space occupied by one half the race and is the preoccupation of the other half, is still one of the great unexplored terrains and worthy of the odd revelation.

The bulk of sex in today's crime novels belongs to *bad* people: rapists, child molesters, serial killers, the most perverse of sex murderers. Their sex acts are specific, personal, and unique; they're dwelt on at length, are related to character and are significant to the plot.

It's true that there is a tendency to deal with the criminal aspect of any sort of behavior, since we are writing crime novels. Thus we have criminal politicians, criminal businessmen, criminal lawyers. But it goes quite beyond that. There is, without doubt, a new puritanism, a group mind that sees sex as one of the forces of evil, to be feared.

CHAPTER 8

Violence

A crime novel without violence is:

a. like smoking pot without inhaling.
b. like sex without orgasm.
c. like a hug without a squeeze.

There are lots of different kinds of violence.

My instinctive classification system divides violence into three types: (1) good fun; (2) satisfying revenge; (3) repulsive/threatening.

The differences have nothing to do with content, they refer to what the readers' attitudes will be. The what and the how of the violence are not distinguishing features; our feelings about the violence are determined almost entirely by the nature of the victim.

The violence in a James Bond novel is quite good fun. In

this scene Bond skis away from the bad guys. A whole troop of them. He skis through an avalanche and loses most of them there. Then suddenly one of them, the guide, shows up, shooting. Now it's going to be a race to the bottom, which is across a parking area and some railroad tracks. Just as James realizes that, he sees an oncoming train and the train is going to get to the crossing just about the time that he will. He puts on all the speed he can. And then:

Hell! A man got out of the black car and was crouching, aiming at him. Bond jinked and jinked again as fire bloomed from the man's hand. But now Bond was on top of him. He thrust hard with the rapier point of ski stick and felt it go through clothing. The man gave a scream and went down. The guide, now only yards behind, yelled something. The great yellow eye of the diesel glared down the tracks, and Bond caught a sideways glimpse of a huge red snow-fan below the headlight that was fountaining the new snow to the right and left of the engine in two white wings. Now! He flashed across the parking place, heading straight at the mound of the embankment and, as he hit, dug both his sticks in to get his skis off the ground and hurled himself forward into the air. There was a brief glimpse of steel rails below, a tremendous thudding in his ears, and a ferocious blast, only yards away, from the train's siren. Then he crashed on to the icy road, tried to stop, failed, and fetched up in an almighty skid against the hard snow wall on the other side. As he did so, there came a terrible scream from behind him, a loud splintering of wood, and the screech of the train's brakes being applied.

At the same time, the spray from the snow-fan, that had now reached Bond, turned pink!

Ian Fleming, *On Her Majesty's Secret Service*

Chester Himes wrote a wonderful series of books in which his fun-filled attitude toward violence is reflected in the names of the heroes—Coffin Ed and Gravedigger Jones—and in the titles themselves—*Cotton Comes to Harlem, Blind Man with a Pistol, The Crazy Kill*. When Quentin Tarantino made his film about fun violence he called it, in homage, *Pulp Fiction*.

In fun violence the bad guys are pretty much ciphers. They may be vivid and colorful in a comic-book way, but they are one-dimensional and soulless.

Donald Westlake, using the pseudonym Richard Stark, wrote a series about an armed robber named Parker. Not to be confused with Spenser books by Parker, Parker books by Stark are quintessential hard-boiled thrillers. The most famous one was *Point Blank*, made into a film with Lee Marvin. One of them, *Slayground*, literally takes place in an amusement park. Parker is trapped there with a bag full of money, and a group of gangsters are going to try to take it away from him.

Here is how some of them are described. Caliato: "He was thirty-eight years old and he knew for a certainty that he'd be running this city before he was fifty. Lozini was top man now, but he was getting old, and already he deferred to Caliato on some issues. . . ." Tony Chaka: "liked cartoons, they were his favorite kind of television, they were the reason he'd sprung for a color set." Benniggio: ". . . an also-ran. He was going to be an also-ran all his life, he was never going to be top of the heap, and by Alfred Benniggio that was just fine." Abadandi and Pulsone, who "were storytellers by nature, Abadandi with recountals of seductions and near seductions . . . Pulsone a teller of movie plots and third-hand anecdotes."

Parker is going to kill or maim all of these people. Do we care? No. We care only how cleverly and coolly he does it.

Note also that Parker is outnumbered and that the people he hurts "started it." The self-justifying cry of every kid in the playground: "But he started it, Mom!"

Satisfying violence is closely related. Except we don't merely take pleasure in the fact that violence is taking place, it's who it's done to that makes us happy. It's the moment when the bad guy gets stomped, mutilated, savaged, whomped, and bomped. It is done to someone who "deserves" it. It's "just deserts," "natural justice," "an eye for an eye." It's a fella "who needed killing." Mickey Spillane and Andrew Vachss, for example, specialize in this.

Repulsive and/or threatening violence is what is done to good people. It has two functions. One is to upset the reader—"Oh, what an awful, nasty thing to happen." The other is to motivate the action—"Oh dear, something must be done about this."

What distinguishes any one of these three from the others is how the writer defines the victim. That is the only thing that separates the three.

A child molester has been buggering little boys. The cop knows it but can't pin it on him. The cop arrests him on some other flimsy charge, gets him sent to a tough prison, and lets it be known what the molester has done. In prison the molester is beaten and gang-raped. We are meant to get a sense of satisfaction from that. The acts are virtually identical, only the victim is switched.

Bad guys do bad things to good people.

Good guys do bad things to bad people.

The gooder the victim, the badder the bad guys.

How do you make a good victim? A good victim has at least some of the conventional virtues. One or two of the following will do: honesty, innocence, kindness, an affectionate nature, cheerful disposition, personal attractiveness, love for others, charity, and so on.

To make victims more sympathetic, they should have a little narrative drive in their lives. It could be a grandmother waiting for her grandchildren to come visit; a teenage girl who's just received an athletic scholarship; a cop in a twelve-step program who's ready to attempt reconciliation with his wife and child; a child who has just come home from a life-threatening operation.

There is one circumstantial difference that also helps to distinguish repulsive/threatening violence: the victim should be defenseless. It can't be a fair fight. Fun violence goes the opposite way; the bad guy victim is bigger and better armed than the good guy. Usually there are more of them as well. In satisfying violence the bad guy is normally untouchable, protected by size, armament, lawyers, power, position, and the inability of the system to deal with him. At the actual moment of stomping he may be defenseless. That's part of the pleasure. Squash him like a bug, like he did to our darling little crippled Judy.

Spend time establishing your bad guys. The bigger they are, the more fun to blow them up. To get that satisfied feeling from hurting them, they must first hurt someone who has been established as an appealing victim, lovable and helpless.

Once you decide the emotional chord that you want to strike, what makes good violence is the same thing that makes good sex: construction, clarity, and, if possible, a sense of freshness.

CHAPTER 9

Finding Material & Characters

We have four basic libraries of material to draw upon for a book: ourselves, the news, other people, and previous books.

All writers draw upon themselves and their experience. One of the basic tricks of both writers and actors is to simply imagine themselves in alternate realities. While the whole of yourself might not be capable of being either a serial killer or an FBI agent, there are parts in each of us that are capable of almost anything. If we look inside ourselves and find the appropriate parts, imagine the inappropriate parts as faded to insignificance, and then place that readjusted persona up against the forces in our plot, we have not only a pretty good character, we have an emotionally felt one as well.

Several writers have said that they are every character in their books.

The news is more important to mystery writers than to other writers because the media spends a lot of time working the same territory—crime: serial killers, robbers, gangsters, gang-bangers, cops, crooked cops, supercops, cops who rescue, cops who answer to 911, American detectives, the FBI, and the Secret Service.

The biggest source of character material is other people. I think they are particularly easy to find for the beginning writer. You live with them. When I wrote my first book I had a lifetime of people hanging around my mind eager to jump right into the pages. There was a waiting list. As you write more books you begin to use them up: some dead, some dismembered, some simply discarded. So later on you have to work harder at it, recycling some of them, changing their age or hair color. Or make new friends—always an arduous task—to base new characters on.

Here's how you do it. You take someone you know and put him or her in radically different circumstances. For example, take your mom, make her earn her living as a hit person. Well, you say, your mom could never be a hit person, she's nurturing, caring, and generally motherly. Now you must alter her character—although you keep her persona intact—in such a way that it is believable that your mom kills people for cash. And possibly for pleasure. There, that's one character.

Next, take the pig who bullied you through high school and make him or her Mr. Big in the crime syndicate. But, you say, Piggy was much too incompetent to boss anything, even the latrine brigade. Now you have two choices—make Piggy a better person or write *The Gang That Couldn't Shoot Straight*.

Now you need some good guys. Let's start with the love interest. Pick someone you have—or have had—a relationship with that left you with a rosy glow—that intrauterine warmth or testosterone haze—and write about that person the way you saw him or her when you were intoxicated on your own hormones.

Next, the protagonist. That's you. As you would be if you

were deadlier, cleaner, better endowed, of a different ethnic persuasion, and clothes hung on you better. Or if you were more intellectual, spoke with a lisp, knew that your parents lied about your real ancestry, could speak three languages, and felt that trial by combat should be the true goal of the Human Potential Movement.

You have lots of friends, enemies, acquaintances, co-workers, lovers, ex-lovers, and in-laws who are just dying to be players in your plots. Thinly disguised or thickly, in featured parts, bits, or as extras, they don't care. Do be a bit cautious about invasion of privacy. Prior to publication you will receive queries from your publisher. If you based a character or characters on a real person in a recognizable way that may cause them demonstrable damage or harm, be completely frank with your publishers' lawyers. Their advice will err on the far side of caution and you can make appropriate changes at that time.

Writing is a very solitary, solipsistic, even onanistic business. The writer—at least this writer—needs contact with the outside world. I do a variety of things to get it. I'm a part-time ski instructor. I have written for my local newspaper, *The Woodstock Times*, and may do so again. I want to write more nonfiction, just to force me into contact with people. Who are not my wife and children. Who are not middle-class bohemian artists, publishers, or agents. If I don't, I suspect I and my writing will dry up and become something thin and brittle and sort of empty.

Then there are other books. All forms of art and entertainment are self-referential. These will be called, if you ever become a literary figure, your influences. But since we are crime writers, let us call it theft, even plagiarism. As with any crime, the point is to do it in such a manner that you profit by it and evade punishment for it. So steal with cheer from Hammett and Chandler, Christie and Conan Doyle. Everyone else has.

John DeSantis, newspaperman and author of *For the Color*

of His Skin, a nonfiction book about the killing of a young African-American male in an Italian-American neighborhood in Brooklyn, and of *The New Untouchables*, about police violence, did me the courtesy of reading this book and suggested that I must not be so quick and casual to recommend theft and plagiarism. There are people who would misunderstand. He's probably right.

Here's what I mean.

When I wrote my first novel I deliberately set out to do an update of the Spade and Marlowe tradition. I asked myself, how would the times have made things different? The classic client was a rich old man with a house on a hill with errant daughters. It seemed to me that in our day and age, individuals had given way to corporations, especially as repositories of big money. I spoke to several people I knew and asked them if they knew of a corporate case or situation that would make good grist for my mystery mill. One of them said: "How about what's happening at Gulf and Western?"

What was happening at G & W, the conglomerate known on Wall Street as Engulf & Devour, which owned Paramount Pictures, among other things, was that an attorney had been charged with misappropriating a significant amount of funds. After several years of fighting it, he pleaded guilty to one felony count. Even though this was a first offense and a white-collar crime, the judge decided to sentence the perpetrator to Attica. Attica is one of those really bad prisons where bad things happen to bad people. Horrid, grotesque things, above and beyond the intentional discomforts and deprivations of incarceration.

This middle-aged, middle-class, white lawyer did not want to go to Attica. He contacted the Securities and Exchange Commission, who had wanted to make a case against G & W for a long, long time, and promised to testify against his own clients if the SEC would keep him out of Attica.

This was a situation loaded with potential. I fictionalized the corporation and the principal players, then I killed the fictional lawyer just as he began to testify. That made it a classical murder mystery, yet clearly a contemporary story. From the detective's side, I felt the primary difference was that where once there was certainty, now there was always ambiguity.

Frank Serpico and Bob Leuci—both NYPD cops who testified against other corrupt cops, both subjects of books that were made into movies—had made a great impression on me. What happened to them? What would life be like afterward for someone who had been through that? So I gave my detective hero that background. But I wanted to make it different. At that time I worked for a political consultant who had once been a corrections officer. This was a variation on the theme, so I made Tony an ex-CO instead of an ex-cop.

This was my first novel. And I knew—from legend—that first novels are always autobiographical. I didn't want this to be too much so, and although I realized the voice and some of the attitudes would be mine, I made the character Sicilian-American to distance him from me. I borrowed his name, Cassella, from a friend. When it came time to do his bio, I knew I wanted him to have parents, strong and influential people in his life. There are stereotypes of Italian and Sicilian-American culture. They have a certain validity. But there, too, I decided to run a variation. I had heard the names Sacco and Vanzetti and Garibaldi. Obviously Italians were not all Corleones. There were intellectuals and radicals and union organizers—a background close to my own family's—and so I plugged that in.

All the women, including the mother, were people I knew. As were many of the bit players.

There it is: snippets and swatches from reality, books, movies, friends, library research, the author's life, the author's fears, the author's wish list. Cut and paste.

There is a toy that consists of three stacked blocks. On each of the four sides there is a picture of an animal—a tiger, a bear, an elephant, a crocodile. There's a post down the center of the blocks so that you can twist them separately and give the tiger's head an elephant belly and crocodile feet. You can put the bear's feet under a crocodile's belly and top it off with an elephant's head. In that way you make your own creature.

CHAPTER 10

Character

Character has been the subject of more confusing, mystifying double talk than any other aspect of writing. Like this:

"The most important element of the mystery novel is character."

"Readers want characters they can root for. Write characters that people can care about."

"Characters are the basic reason people read books."

"You have to write good, strong characters."

"A good novel is character driven."

"The reason the reader cares what happens next is because of the author's skill at making characters."

"The most important thing is to write characters who are real people."

All of these are untrue. Or often untrue. Or sometimes untrue. Worse, they don't contain a clue as to how to achieve what they're talking about. Nor—for the most part—do the essays that they have been taken from.

The point of this book is to demystify the process and give you some tools to use. We're going to lay it out this way.

1. How to make characters
2. How to make characters function in books
3. Symbiosis of plot & character
4. Character as narrative drive
5. Signs & symbols
6. Style
7. Character first
8. The mystery of compelling characters

HOW TO MAKE CHARACTERS

Method 1: Gestalt

The first and simplest way is to take a person, as a whole, a gestalt, the way you think of a person, and write him or her. Usually you use people you know. They're ready at hand, as a package, with a look, a style, an age, a background, patterns of conduct, and some juicy anecdotes.

Sherlock Holmes, or at least his most distinctive trait, the business of deducing a whole person's life by looking at the mud on his shoes and the callus on his third finger and the stitching in his britches, was modeled on one of Conan Doyle's professors at Edinburgh University.

The professor was not a consulting detective. Conan Doyle took the "character" and put him to new uses. At this point you hold an image of your professor in your head and imagine how he would behave running across the moors chasing after a giant hound.

Frequently one person is not enough. So you put the head of one on the body of another.

George Smiley was based on two Oxford dons. One, I am told, had Smiley's persona, the other was the actual spy.

These people, whom you are gracious enough to reemploy as characters, need not come from life. They may come from dreams, books, films, wish fulfillment.

I read an account of one writer who looks at magazines for photographs of interesting faces and for people who might fit roles that she needs in her book, then tacks them on the wall above the computer screen and imagines them from their appearance.

Method 2: From a list

Warning: the following charts and lists look intimidating. Possibly overwhelming.

They are tools. Tools are meant to be used by the craftsman, not vice versa. No matter how big a hammer is, it can't hit anything without you. Tools do not dictate when they should be used; the craftsman determines that.

The first chart comes from an article by Lary Crews on writing mysteries that's posted in the CompuServe Crime Forum library. It is quite astute and useful. He likes to do extensive character profiles, ten- to fifty-page biographies, that include:

- Birthplace
- Nationality
- Morals
- Ambitions

- Education
- Character flaws
- Habitual mannerisms
- Fears
- Frustrations
- Taste in sexual partners

The *Concise Oxford Textbook of Psychiatry* (Michael Gelder, Dennis Gath, Richard Mayou, Oxford University Press, 1994) has a guide for a psychiatrist's first interview with a patient. It's a very handy form for character bios.

Name, age, address
Informants & their relationship to the patient
Family history
Personal history
Past illness
Personality
Drugs, alcohol, tobacco

HISTORY OF THE PRESENT CONDITION
  Patient's description of the problem
  Details of the nature of the problem and present severity of
    the symptoms
  Systematic enquiry about other relevant problems and symptoms
  Onset and course of symptoms and of problems

THE FAMILY HISTORY
  Parents:
    Age (now or at death)
    Occupation
    Personality
    Relationship with the patient

Siblings
  Age (now or at death/cause of death)
  Occupation
  Personality
  Relationship with the patient
Social position
Atmosphere in the home
Mental disorder in other members of the (extended) family,
  abuse of alcohol & drugs

PERSONAL HISTORY
Mother's pregnancy & the birth
Early development
Childhood
  separations
  emotional problems
  illnesses
Schooling & higher education
Occupations
Sexual relationships
Menstrual history
Marriage
Children
Social circumstances
Forensic history
Past medical history
Past psychiatric history

GENERAL APPEARANCE
Physique, hair, makeup, clothing
Facial expression
Posture
Movements
Social behavior

During the interview the psychiatrist would note:

> Speech pattern
> Mood
> Depersonalization & derealization
> Disorders of thinking
> Abnormalities of perception
>   Illusions
>   Cognitive functions
>   Attention and concentration
>   Intelligence
>   Insight

With a slight shift in orientation and some minor translations, this is very evocative of a client's initial consultation with a detective. Meet the Sternwoods at the start of *The Big Sleep*. Raymond Chandler's thumbnail sketches, the first time he has us meet a new character, would be a psychiatrist's delight.

Having gotten the history and observed the patient, the psychiatrist now prepares a formulation.

> Statement of the problem
>
> The differential diagnosis
>   [There is frequently more than one problem, with the symptoms overlapping or masking each other, e.g., alcoholism and schizophrenia.]
>   Primary, secondary: evidence for differentiation
>
>   Aetiology [causes of the disease]
>   Predisposing: What makes the client vulnerable

> Precipitating: What brought the disease or episode on
> Maintaining: What keeps it going
>
> Further investigations
>   As appropriate
>
> Treatment plan
>   Drugs
>   Psychological treatment
>   Social measures
>
> Prognosis

This is analogous to what the detective does to sum up that first client meeting.

[The Problem:]
Spade said: "Miss Wonderly's sister ran away from New York with a fellow named Floyd Thursby. They're here. Miss Wonderly has seen Thursby and has a date with him tonight. Maybe he'll bring the sister with him. The chances are he won't. Miss Wonderly wants us to find the sister and get her away from him and back home."

[The Treatment Plan:]
"We shouldn't have any trouble with it. It's simply a matter of having a man at the hotel this evening to shadow him away when he leaves, and shadow him until he leads us to your sister."

[The Prognosis:]
". . . If she comes with him, and you persuade her to return with you, so much the better. Otherwise—if she

doesn't want to leave him after we've found her—well, we'll find a way of managing that."
        Dashiell Hammett, *The Maltese Falcon*

Gelder, Gath, and Mayou also recommend life charts, set up like this:

year	age	Events	Physical Illness	Psychiatric Disorder
1957	born	premature	jaundice	n/a
1958	1	walking	chicken pox	nervous
1959	2	etc.	etc.	etc.

There will be a line for each year. Right up through whatever the present moment is. If the subject were forty, there would be forty lines, though many of them might only list the date and the patient's age.

This can easily be adapted to the way you view people.

year	age	Events	Psychological Effect	Relationship to Story
1957	born	female circumcision	trauma, sexual dysfunction	religious rift in family

Or, adapted specifically for mysteries:

year	age	Events	Relation to Crime	How It Is Discovered
1957	born	illegitimate	secret heir	old nursemaid

This last chart can be a complete outline for certain kinds of stories.

In fiction, as in real life, the uncovering of the personal and public history of the victim and of the chief suspects is very frequently the primary activity of the investigation. In the Lew Archer books by Ross Macdonald, the story is always an exploration of the family history. In the Dr. Delaware books by Jonathan Kellerman, in which the investigator is a psychiatrist, the story is the uncovering of a personal history.

In my first two books, *No One Rides for Free* and *You Get What You Pay For*, I did business histories, and uncovering those was the spine of the story.

These look immense and daunting. But by doing them you will discover a lot about the characters and about the story. You will in fact write things that will end up on the final pages. It's also a great thing to do when you get stuck.

The only drawback that I can think of is that, having done the work, you may want to keep more than you should.

Method 3: Creating characters to suit the action

Character is action. People are what they do.

If someone is going to kill, he needs to have the means (ability), motive (desire), opportunity (a role in life that places him next to the victim), temperament, and morality.

If someone is going to help the investigator, he must have the knowledge to help, which will be dictated by his life role, the ability to help, and a reason to help.

If the plot could use someone who knows vital information but is inclined to withhold it, forcing the investigator to do something else to manipulate him, that suggests a different manufacture.

This is one of the strongest and most vital ways to create a character.

Method 4: Create characters to suit the theme or the subject matter

The theme of *The Godfather* is the Sicilian immigrant experience. Mario Puzo started the story with a baker, an undertaker, and Frank Sinatra. Each of them is having difficulties with life in the New World and must turn to Don Corleone, the Godfather, to help in his special way.

Gillian Farrell is an actress who worked as a PI in New York. Her life was optioned to be a film before she herself had done a book based on her experiences. A script was written by someone else. It wasn't very good. The reason it didn't work, she thought, was because it was written about someone who was a detective. Her story was about an actor who also detected. Later, the star who was going to play her character got divorced from the man who owned the studio; the producer, who was the nephew of the man who owned the production company, got interested in something else; and the rights reverted and Gillian got her own shot at turning her life into a story. She wanted to do it in a way that would deal with being an actor. She came up with a story in which the three major characters were actresses: a good and idealistic one who couldn't get work; a terrible one who worked all the time and made piles of money; and one who, beaten down by the constant abuse to her self-esteem (which is an essential part of the aspiring actor's life), had become a drug user and a sexual semiprofessional.

In actuality we usually use a combination of all four approaches.

Any one of them, or any mixture, can lead to good results and to lousy ones.

HOW TO MAKE CHARACTERS FUNCTION IN BOOKS

Character is a set of walls, like the four walls of a squash court. They are the boundaries of what a fictional person can do.

Things happen and a person reacts. He cannot have a reaction outside the walls of "character." For the most part the hero cannot, due to his moral nature, gun down a defenseless man. This wall of his character makes him appealing but, in certain emergencies, limits his range of action. In the film version of *Carlito's Way* this virtue is the weakness that leads directly to the hero's death. Sonny Corleone can't control his temper. His enemies know it and use it to lead him to his death. Michael Corleone can't walk away from his Sicilian code of justice and vengeance and family. Sam Spade won't play the sap for anyone.

Once you have "established" a character, once those walls are up, you can't blithely walk through them. You must have characters respond in character, i.e., stay within the walls. If a character does something just for the plot, without regard to his personality or nature, we lose a certain feeling toward the book. This is usually described in literary terms—the characters are "wooden" or "one-dimensional" or "subservient to the plot." The error is not in making a character do something, but the way the writer has him do it. The disappointment on the part of the reader does not come from a "literary" sensibility or critic's code.

The problem is actually that the reader feels that the writer is not playing the game very well.

This is simpler to understand if we think of characters more in terms of abilities and disabilities. George Smiley is patient and cunning, fat, elderly, and unimposing. If John

Le Carré had Smiley solve a case by suddenly donning an Aqua-Lung, swimming the channel to East Germany, killing the deadly guard dogs in hand-to-hand combat, shooting his way into the dacha of the head of the KGB, then making his escape by seducing the female security staff, we would throw up our hands and walk away. That's not the way you play the game.

However difficult the problem is, the writer must find a way to solve it that remains within the boundaries that have been set. What happens if a chess player suddenly insists that his bishop can move over pawns like a knight? Or if a tennis player brings in a machine to hit his serves for him? A baseball player uses a corked bat, or a boxer puts lead in his gloves. It's the rules that make the game.

It's moderately harder to visualize this in books because the rules are not laid out in a common rule book. They change book by book; and worse, the writer makes up his own rules in each book. Nonetheless, it is a game, the rules exist, and breaking them blows the game away.

Yes, there are times when people will go through the walls. But in order to do so you must go to great pains to demonstrate that their existence was an illusion and the characters are not who we thought they were—perhaps not who they themselves thought they were. Or you must make them change in order to go through the walls, or make them pay the price for betraying their own character. Once erected, you can't simply ignore the boundaries.

Pardon me while I move the metaphor over to the tennis court. Tennis references are more widely known than squash ones.

You're playing against a pro. You don't have much of a serve, you have so-so ground strokes and a great drop shot, you're forty years old and your conditioning is above average for your age. That's your "character," your strengths and limitations on the tennis court.

You're playing for very high stakes. Ten thousand dollars a point.

If you win, you can pay for the operation that will save the life of your ten-year-old daughter, the sweetest, brightest thing on all of God's good earth.

If you lose, you lose everything. Home, car, family, future earnings. And your beloved child. You will have to stand there, helpless, and watch her die before your eyes, knowing that somehow you should have found a way to save her.

Ready? Put on your sneakers and shorts, pick up your racket and balls, and get out there.

Here is what you can*not* do. You can't develop Boris Becker's serve. Or John McEnroe's net game. Or Andre Agassi's ground strokes. Those are physical impossibilities. And literary ones.

But what you might do, if you're desperate enough, is, when you shake hands at the start of the game, break the pro's thumb. Or you might try to explain to him exactly how wonderful your daughter is and engage his sympathy. You might offer him your body, hire goons to beat him up the night before, slip lethal mushrooms into his omelet, tell him you'll kill his mother if he wins, drop acid on the strings of his only racket.

You might choose to do your best, fight the good fight, and lose respectably. Or whimper and cry and lose disrespectfully.

That's the game of character. Limits. Potentials. Choices. Pressure. Solutions that don't exceed the limits but make use of the potentials in ways that the reader didn't think of first.

SYMBIOSIS OF PLOT & CHARACTER

If George Smiley had never been recruited by the Circus and had remained a German scholar at one of the more obscure Oxford colleges, he would *not* have been an "interesting" and "compelling" character. He would have been, I expect, rather a bore, and a dusty one at that, with the irritating habit of having every sentence trail off into inaudibility at the end so that even other doddering dons would only pretend to understand what the hell he was talking about.

Having conceived of a character, it is the author's job to find situations to test his mettle. Take his abilities to the limit, but not beyond.

Conversely, if you start with a situation, you should employ characters of the appropriate dimensions. You don't use Superman to solve a simple burglary.

Give it to an octogenarian with brittle bones who suffers from occasional incontinence and who requires medication for her high blood pressure. Then make her go around the neighborhood confronting roving groups of bored, vicious, nasty teenagers. That's an adventure and a test of character.

When you're working, you go back and forth. Characters can be adjusted. Plots can be adjusted. If you simply cannot find a way for a character to commit the act that the plot requires, you can go back and alter the person's nature. You can take the time to write a scene wherein the person changes or an unexpected but consistent dimension is revealed. Or you can change the plot. In fact, you will use all of these solutions.

CHARACTER AS NARRATIVE DRIVE

Lary Crews, in the CompuServe essay, says:

> *The essence of character, for literary purposes, is a character's ability to CARE about something; to feel that SOMETHING is important . . . major or minor, disastrous or trivial. . . . The crucial issue is that . . . it's strong enough to move them.*

The more clearly articulated, indicated, and demonstrated a person's needs are, the more "vivid" your character is. This applies to heroes and villains, major characters and minor ones.

We choose the details of character by what moves them. Suppose that you have written thirty-page biographies for your characters and you have filled out psychiatric worksheets on all the major and some of the minor ones. When you write them into the story you start drowning in detail. How do you pick and choose? What stays in? What goes out?

We use the principle of narrative drive. What will move the person? What will limit action?

Many people, for example, are really, truly concerned with what the neighbors will think. Some are fiercely conventional. It is possible to twist yourself far out of shape, to assault your spouse and to beat your children, in order to convince the world that there is nothing odd about you at all. Given the situation, this drive will either be a restriction on the characters' ability to act or impel them to act.

If that aspect of the character is relevant to the story, you must show it, you must find details that make repression vivid.

Meet Moose Malloy from Raymond Chandler's *The Big*

Sleep. He's got the opposite problem. He's first seen looking up at a neon sign of a "dime and dice emporium" called Florian's in a racially mixed section of L.A.:

> He was looking up at the dusty windows with a sort of ecstatic fixity of expression, like a hunky immigrant catching his first sight of the Statue of Liberty. He was a big man but not more than six feet five inches tall and not wider than a beer truck.
>
> . . . He wore a shaggy borsalino hat, a rough gray sports coat with white golf balls on it for buttons, a brown shirt, a yellow tie, pleated gray flannel slacks and alligator shoes with white explosions on the toes. From his outer breast pocket cascaded a show handkerchief of the same brilliant yellow as his tie. There were a couple of coloured feathers tucked into the band of his hat, but he didn't really need them. Even on Central Avenue, not the quietest dressed street in the world, he looked about as inconspicuous as a tarantula on a slice of angel food.
>
> . . . He stood like a statue, and after a long time he smiled.

Moose goes in. A person comes flying out. Marlowe looks in.

> A hand I could have sat in came out of the dimness and took hold of my shoulder and squashed it to a pulp. Then the hand moved through the doors and casually lifted me up a step.

Moose can't understand why there was an African-American—a "smoke"—in the joint. Marlowe tries to explain that the place has changed. New clientele.

> "Don't say that, pal," the big man purred softly, like four tigers after dinner. "Velma used to work here. Little

Velma . . . Yeah," he said, "Little Velma. I ain't seen her in eight years."

We have a pretty fair idea that Moose is a man more responsive to his own inner vision than driven by social conventions.

SIGNS & SYMBOLS

Outward show is the manifestation of inner drives.

The way Moose Malloy dresses is a direct reflection of the way he views the world and the way he feels it is correct for him to conduct himself in it.

The very rigidity of the old FBI dress code was supposed to be symbolic of the rectitude within.

In our daily lives we make instant deductions of who people are by their dress, deportment, grooming, physical attractiveness, apparent physical condition, manner of speech, facial expression, manner of standing or moving. We decide if we are interested, disinterested, frightened, attracted. We estimate how to handle them should contact take place.

We continue to do so even as we get to know them better. Even if we know that the image is at odds with the reality, we may never entirely cease to react to the signs and symbols.

These signals are not necessarily accurate or true. Any man who has spent a lot of time chasing women knows that a woman who employs flagrant erotic symbols, from scarlet nails to fetish heels, is often completely uninterested in actual sex. And if she has sex, she may not like it very much. Women have the reverse experience. Men will appear to be one way, single, for example, and then turn out to have a very different reality.

A good con man must master the mannerisms and symbols of sincerity and probity.

All people live inside full body masks. What we see of people and hear from them is their ongoing statement: "This is the way I think I should look; this is who I want to be; this is how I want to be seen." There is a degree of connection between who a person is and his mask. There is a degree of disconnection. The relationship varies more than shoe size.

The relationship between the mask and the inner self is under varying degrees of control. Rage, love, contempt, desire, boredom, and a host of other feelings and conditions are routinely covered up. People pretend to feelings: they fake anger, love, understanding, happiness, satisfaction, weakness, distress, and illness. They also pretend to conditions: erudition, literacy, wealth, status, health, contentment, job competence, physical skills.

The disguise of the inner self and the creation of the image are frequently unconscious and often compulsive. The mask maker may not be in control of his doing it, nor even aware of its being done. People often believe deeply and passionately in their masks. They will often become extremely defensive, hostile, and angry when confronted with the discord between the self they believe in and the self they are. Denial is a powerful thing.

At the same time that every person is engaged in image creation, every viewer is involved in acts of perception. These are processes of induction and deduction. Some viewers see through body masks and past gestures of distraction better than others. In part, this is a talent, like the ability to watch other athletes on the tennis court or basketball court and see where they are actually going with the ball. Part of this is practice.

All viewers have blind spots. Some of those blindnesses are semipermanent, part of the viewer's condition. Some are temporary. Emotion creates blind spots, especially fear and desire. In *Tinker, Tailor, Soldier, Spy* the double agent inside the Circus makes love to George Smiley's wife and makes sure that George knows about it, in order to cloud Smiley's mind, and prevent him from seeing past it to the real betrayal.

Lovers in lust don't see flaws in their beloved; people possessed by greed can't see the most obvious con games; true believers can't recognize the sins of their messiahs.

Two frequently asked questions in police procedurals, real and fictional—Patricia Cornwell's *All That Remains*, for example—are: How did the killer get into the victim's apartment? Or how did he talk the victim into going with him? In other words, how did the killer stylize himself, what symbols did he use, to convince the victim to trust him?

There was recently a front-page obituary of an obscure jazz musician who lived in the Pacific Northwest. Married and the father of—if I remember correctly—several adopted children, two of whom were boys. Upon the musician's death, it turned out that he was a woman who had disguised herself as a man back in the days when women were not acceptable in the world of jazz. She maintained that disguise for some thirty or forty years, even with her own children.

Sign, symbol, illusion, delusion, full body mask.

STYLE

Tom Wolfe (*The Right Stuff, Bonfire of the Vanities, The Electric Kool-Aid Acid Test*) is one of my favorite writers. He has a thesis, both implicit and articulated, that style is substance.

The Right Stuff is a work of New Journalism, a true story written with the tools of a novelist, dialogue, plot, characters, subplots. It is the story of the first American astronauts.

They were recruited from the top military pilots. Men who landed fighter planes on aircraft carrier decks at night, flew bombing and surveillance missions over hostile territory, tested experimental aircraft. Jobs that required great physical ability, intelligence, commitment, courage, luck, and something more, that uncataloged quality called "the right stuff."

The right stuff was the ability to sit in the cockpit of a jet aircraft that was spiraling out of control when the ejectors had jammed—so the pilot was reasonably certain of imminent death—and still continue to perform the recommended procedures, stay on the radio reporting what he had done and its result, never showing a sign of panic, by word or deed. It was best to speak in a distinct and measured manner, and a touch of West Virginia drawl was considered to add a dash of style.

That is to say, the right stuff was cool, but more than that, it was style. It was grace under pressure, it was Cyrano's white plume, it was panache.

The rate of death from accidents for career navy pilots was 23 percent, a figure that did not include death in combat. The mortality rate for test pilots in certain programs was significantly higher. What were these men taking the risk of dying for, if not to prove that they had "the right stuff"? Boyz in the 'hood are not killing and dying for survival or food for their families or for getting rich. They're doing it to show that they have style, cool, something hipper than manliness, "the right stuff."

Style—image, attitude—is not shallow. It is pervasive and profound. Men and women stay together in marriages because they are concerned with what others will think. Women will starve themselves to death to appear slender. Immigrant children work twice as hard at school, not merely in the belief that good grades mean good jobs, but to prove they are as good as anyone else, perhaps even better, and to make their parents proud. Litigators and athletes fight to win because of the way they imagine other people will think about them. They fear losing, even when there is no profit either way, because they fear for their image, they fear that others will look upon them with pity or contempt.

In *Bonfire of the Vanities* all the characters act out of their concern for their self-image and for their image in the eyes of others.

In the end, Sam Spade sends Brigid O'Shaugnessy up because he won't "play the sap." This is not a moral decision. It is a style choice.

Toxic Leaks

This is an acting term. I learned it from my wife, who learned it from someone else. A toxic leak is that line of dialogue or moment or act in which the character's inner life leaks out from behind his carefully constructed mask, and if we are paying attention, we see who he really is.

> *Ranks of weapons, together with some jewelry, pots, and ritual objects were labeled and mounted on shelves inside glass cases which lined three walls of the room. . . .*
>
> *"I study one people at a time," he explained. "It gives me something to do since I retired, and I find it enthralling. Did you know that in the Fiji Islands the men used to fatten women like cattle and eat them?"*
>
> *His eyes gleamed and I had a suspicion that part of the pleasure he derived from primitive peoples lay in contemplation of their primitive violences.*
>
> Dick Francis, *Dead Cert*

When Tom Ripley, in Patricia Highsmith's *The Amazing Mr. Ripley*, sneaks into Dickie Greenleaf's room and tries on Dickie's clothes, it's a toxic leak. When Dickie catches him at it, he recognizes it as such, and realizes that Tom is exposing something weird. He doesn't perceive that Tom is exposing something lethal.

This is not the same as the moment when a person lets slip something that "only the killer could have known." That's a mechanical moment, though in the plot they may serve the same purpose.

Unbelievable Characters

My doctor, who is a very, very unusual person, says, "I'm Dutch. In my country people say, 'Just be yourself, that will be strange enough.' "

It's pretty hard to create a character weirder than the real world: Jeffrey Dahmer, Howard Hughes, Lee Harvey Oswald. Don't be afraid of weirdness, oddity, eccentricity, compulsiveness, the unorthodox, the bizarre, outlandish, alien, exotic. Weirdness does not create unbelievability.

On the other hand, it's really easy to put people on the page in such a way that we don't believe in them or that we think they're there just for effect. It's necessary to explain how these stranger-than-fiction people manage to exist. If you put a Jeffrey Dahmer in your book, you have to describe a world that can walk right by him, day after day, death after death, and never notice.

Spenser, the Robert Parker character, can kill four, five, ten people in a shoot-out and the cops just shrug. Boston's not that way, but Spenser-world is. It's not a hard leap to make, given the genre. It's a rather conventional one, in fact.

But what Parker can't do is describe the rest of the world with Joseph Wambaugh realism. James Bond inhabits a James Bond world. It's not real, but it's consistent.

CHARACTER FIRST

Between the first and second draft of this I read a novel called *Fence Jumpers*, by Robert Leuci. It's a New York cops-and-mobster story, and in my opinion the best Mafia book since *The Godfather*.

For whatever reasons, maybe because I was paying attention, I finally *felt* a book as character driven. There are three main characters and a bunch of semi-main characters, and they just kind of bang around the world of cops and crooks until they crash into something they can't bounce off of and things go smash.

There's a plot. Mostly it consists of putting these guys in the same pot from birth and keeping them in it while the pressure mounts.

Cop novels and crime novels—insofar as those categories denote something distinct from mystery and detective novels—have more room to be character driven.

In the contemporary cop novel, invented by Joseph Wambaugh (*The New Centurions*, *The Blue Knight*, *The Choirboys*, *The Glitter Dome*, *The Black Marble*, *The Delta Star*, etc.), crime is no longer an anomaly, the story is no longer "solve this crime and life will return to orderliness." Crime is a given—put this perp away and two more assholes show up tomorrow and besides the ADA is gonna screw the pooch and the scumbag's gonna walk anyway and if the ADA is good and puts the case right, the judge'll be havin' a serious case of PMS and throw the whole thing out just so's she can go home, have a hot bath. So it's not so much about solving this f'n case, it's about living in the sewer of contemporary Western civilization and seeking psychic survival. Today's cop novel is about how cops feel about what they do, how they cope, and what happens when they fail to.

There is a type of crime novel, like the works of Jim Thompson (*The Getaway*, *The Killer Inside Me*, *The Grifters*, *Pop. 1280*), James M. Caine (*Double Indemnity*, *The Postman Always Rings Twice*), and Patricia Highsmith (*Strangers on a Train*, the Ripley novels), in which dark forces dominate people and drive them to act. They are bombs waiting to explode, characters in search of a situation that will turn into a plot.

If you wish to start from character, rather than situation or plot, then you manipulate the circumstances. You create plots that bring out the best and the worst in the people.

Just as we have to take care to make characters substantive in a plot-driven novel, we have to take care not to make our plots too thin. The things that happen have to seem natural and reasonable in that fictional world. A key plot point in *Fence Jumpers* occurs when one of the cops sees the mob guy make a phone call from a pay phone and then is able to find out the number and person he called. The cop has the mob guy under surveillance. It's logical for him to be watching and paying attention. Mob guys worry about being wire-tapped and overheard, but one could easily fail to think that being seen making a phone call from a safe pay phone would be a fatal slip.

It all might start with a coincidence. In fact, they often rely on coincidence, but if it does, we should have a sense that given the characters, it would have happened anyway. Differently perhaps, with a change in cast and even a different denouement. But it would have happened.

Bruno slammed his palms together. "Hey! Cheeses what an idea! We murder for each other, see? I kill your wife and you kill my father! We met on a train, see, and nobody knows we know each other! Perfect alibis! Catch?"
Patricia Highsmith, *Strangers on a Train*

Villains

Lots of men would like to be gangsters. Only a few do it.

What is it about them that allows, or compels, them to live by the gun, while others say "I wish" but go off to the office or punch in at the factory?

What aspects of their personality affect the kind of gangster they become? What parts of them seem incongruous with what they do?

The impulses to kill and steal, to cheat and rob, to extort and blackmail, to rape and control, to beat and mutilate, exist to some degree in most of us. These are the drives outward. In some people they are stronger than in others.

Inhibitions—empathy, guilt, ideals, morality, fear, etc.—are forces of control; they press inward.

One way to enter your villains is to get in touch with the raptures of rage, the righteousness of the bully, the pleasures of acting out the cravings of the id. Imagine what it would be like to be free of the forces that shut you down and close you in. Tune in to the feeling of letting things rip.

Often the serial killer, the rapist, the child molester, the shoplifter, the drug addict, know they are wrong and go through a cycle of repression, craving, giving in to temptation, and remorse that is identical to the cycle that dieters go through when they know there is a chocolate cake waiting for them in the refrigerator.

Sometimes criminality is a matter of opportunity. There

were no Caucasian or Negro nicotine addicts before the European contact with the Americas. The underlying theory of the enforcement of vice laws is to remove opportunity. The foolish-sounding cliché of a good child whose only fault was to have bad companions has an element of truth to it. Even bad children don't learn to burgle, rob, and prostitute themselves by social osmosis. They need guidance, teaching, and support. A Mafia organization needs a whole community to exist in and to draw talent from. A latent gangster in Duluth might have trouble realizing his full potential.

A successful crime creates learned behavior. Classically, the serial killer stumbles into his first murder. But he learns that he likes the reality of it. A lot. He also learns a vastly more terrifying lesson: that he can get away with it.

Villains are constructed like any other character. They are usually constructed with a purpose in mind. Vicious villains are there to draw us into the story by making us feel they must be stopped or that their crimes must be avenged. Minor villains—henchmen, for example—are very often cartoons of badness so that the hero can have fun blowing them away. Major villains are there to test the hero to the utmost.

THE MYSTERY OF COMPELLING CHARACTERS

Don't try to do everything that's been discussed in this chapter. Especially not all at once. These are things to think about, some devices to get you started, theories to go to when what you do doesn't work or when you want to go an extra step.

Much is made of the ability to write "compelling characters," "characters we care about," and "characters who draw us into the story," as an important, if not *the* important, literary quality.

Ninety percent of it is a simple variation of narrative drive. Tell the reader what the character wants and why he wants it, and what makes it so damn important. Explain that both success and failure have awesome consequences. Then show the reader what the character will do in order to obtain what he wants and what he will endure rather than surrender what is important to him.

That is attainable through craft and hard work.

CHAPTER 11

Heroes & Heroines

The hero or heroine is the person at the center of the book. Be that Sherlock Holmes or the Godfather or Parker the robber or the Killer Inside Me.

Aside from that, heroes and heroines are characters, just like any other. The same rules apply. The same tools are available for creating them.

Heroes and heroines are neither good nor bad in terms of conventional morality. They are good and bad in the terms you—the writer—set in your universe.

We each have a head full of heroes and heroines. It can be yourself, someone you want to borrow from real life, someone you steal out of a movie or a book or Greek mythology and vary ever so slightly by changing the gender or skin color or age.

Conventional wisdom says that an active hero is better than a passive one. This is true.

THE DETECTIVE HERO

When people discuss "characters," and especially heroes, there is a great concentration on characteristics. They are often very vivid and they seem to matter, but I would hazard a guess that they matter far less than they appear to.

When I think of various protagonists as people—off the case, outside of the adventure—I don't know if I'm particularly interested in John Grisham's lawyers or Miss Marple or Hercule Poirot. And I can't say I believe in V. I. Warshawski or Dr. Delaware. Or Philip Marlowe, for that matter. I wouldn't say that I rooted for the Killer Inside Me. Though I do, rather, for Tom Ripley.

However, if we think of character as action, if people are what they do, then we can begin to get a handle on the matter. Travis McGee may or may not be your idea of a great guy, but what he does is great, as in greatly interesting.

Travis has a lot of cute stuff around him. He lives on a houseboat in Fort Lauderdale. It's called the *Busted Flush* because he won it in a poker game. He has a Rolls-Royce that someone before him had cut down and made into a pickup truck. It's painted bright blue and he calls it Mrs. Agnes. He's an ex–football player. He's real physical, though sensitive and well read. The world's longest-running house party is on the boat next to him, which belongs to a guy with a colorful moniker, the Alabama Tiger. People who don't like Travis find him long-winded and pretentious and sexist.

Travis makes his living as a "recovery expert." If somebody has had something taken, he'll go after it. He keeps 50 percent of what he gets back. Obviously if his clients could get their things back some less expensive way, through the police or the courts, they would.

I think that everything else except how he makes his living could change and he would still be a "compelling" character.

It's not what he does when he's sitting still, at home or at your dinner party, that's intriguing. It's what he does when a widow comes to him and says: "They killed my husband and stole everything he had; now my two children and I are destitute. The people who have done this are beyond the recourse of normal justice—they are clever, ruthless, amoral, powerful, connected, devious, and scary."

You or I might say, "Jeez, honey, I'm awful sorry, have a drink," or "Let me give you the name of a good lawyer," or "Have you tried social services?" But not Trav. He says, Let's get it back.

Now, McGee has to figure out how the crime was done, who really did it, and who has the money. That's only step one. Step two is conceiving a daring and ingenious plan to get it back. Step three is to do it: scam the scammers, con the con people, rob the robbers, and if it comes down to it, *mano a mano*, kill the killers.

If we think of character as having the mind that can think up those counterscams, having the presence and the cool to pull them off, the guts and the physical capabilities to play it out in the face of death, then we have the beginning of how this character thing might work.

The hero in a Dick Francis novel is a stripped-down and Anglicized Travis McGee. He's no party animal and certainly no womanizer (he can comfortably go without sex longer than most people can go without visiting their dental hygienist). But when he comes up against bad people—who are beyond the control of the law—he, by golly, stands up to them, figures out who they are, exactly what they're doing, how they're doing it, then comes up with a plan to bring them down and get back what the people they've harmed are owed. Plus he has the guts and physical capability to execute the plan.

Bernie Rhodenbarr, the thief-hero of a series by Larry Block, does things—in his hero mode—that are sort of, kinda like, what Francis's ex-jockeys do (most of Dick Francis's protagonists are ex-jockeys, as he is) and what Travis McGee does. Bernie usually gets involved from a less morally pure position. He'll be stealing a painting for a client, stumble on a corpse, and realize that he's been framed. But once that happens, he comes up with ingenious, daring ways to solve the problem. He does so out of that grab bag of characteristics, talents, abilities, and limitations called *self*. And, because he must, he executes the plan in the face of fearful opposition.

Nero Wolfe is an agoraphobic, grotesquely overweight gourmet-glutton who cultivates orchids. These could easily become tedious trivialities. But what they do is raise the stakes of his particular game. The constraints of his compulsions, the walls of his character, are so great that he shouldn't be able to solve anything more than a crossword puzzle. How can a man who won't leave his apartment, who refuses to miss a meal, and who requires lots of money to maintain his peculiar lifestyle support it by being a brilliantly successful detective?

ASSEMBLING THE HERO
(LET ME CONTRADICT MYSELF AGAIN)

It is clear, from the market, from my own reactions, from other readers, that the hero's lifestyle is important. We seem to take great delight in these trappings of character. At mystery conventions I hear things like, "My hero is special because he always consults his mother-in-law about his cases and he has a mynah bird that he calls Donald Duck." "My heroine is a graduate student in computer science and she drives a Volvo with a dent and no one's ever had a Volvo driver before." "My heroine is the first woman Formula One driver and she always has to solve her cases between laps." They're not entirely off the mark.

If you've read lots of crime fiction, you probably have some feelings and ideas about what you would like in your protagonist and what you wouldn't like. If you like reading about people with pets, give your hero a pet. If you're annoyed that the typical detective hero is a loner, give him attachments, a family.

You yourself have certain traits and types of knowledge and attitudes and social groupings and points of reference that you're used to carrying around with you, that are at hand and easy to grab. Unless there are compelling reasons otherwise, that's probably what you should make your hero out of.

What are compelling reasons otherwise?

Theme is one. The subject of *American Hero* is war. Though the war happens offstage, it still meant that the hero should have been a soldier and it suggested that he should have liked Vietnam and studied the art of warfare.

Lots of heroes are created for their special powers: weapons experts, knowledge of martial arts secrets unknown to mere mortals in the West, computer wizardry, psychiatric pharmacology, anthropology, forensic pathology.

Some are created to be unsentimental, others to have appealing depths of feeling.

Some are fantasy figures: of revenge, sexual conquest, getting out of the house, driving fast cars, spitting in the face of the establishment, asserting the power of the establishment over the punks who are ruining life as we wish we knew it.

HERO: ODYSSEUS OR CIPHER?

The old conventional wisdom, which is the opposite of the new conventional wisdom, is that the hero should be a cipher. A sort of investigative tool stuck in a human body. An

eye, an ear, and a computer where the hypothalamus is supposed to be. He is the seer, the viewer, the unraveler.

It is the villain and the victim and the people of their
messy world that have all the passion and confusion and
quirks and history and pain. This is the tradition of Miss
Marple, Hercule Poirot, Nero Wolfe, Perry Mason, and a
thousand others of that ilk. It's less obvious, but hard-boiled
dicks can also function this way. The detective's role in the
story is to get the facts, sort them out, and see justice done.
His role in the book is to be a tour bus. We slip inside him
and look out the windows of his eyes as he glides through the
world of the crime, peeling back the layers, revealing the
secrets, and showing us what life is like among poisonous
middle-class spouses, desperate gutter pimps, even bulimic
princesses.

Closely allied with the choice between a neutral or involved hero are two more options: Is the "case" a personal
matter or a professional one? Is the journey toward truth also
a personal journey for the hero?

There are lots of stories in which the detective takes on
the case for a friend, aging aunt, cousin, buddy, old lover,
new lover. And there are advisers to writers who say that's the
way it should be, that it's necessary to up the ante by making
it "personal." I don't think there are clear-cut advantages or
indications either way. Travis McGee started out taking
cases for profit, not for sentiment. As the years went on, that
hard edge disappeared and emotion took center stage. Either
the author or his fans must have preferred that, though I
didn't, and when my turn came, it inspired me to keep
putting money center stage no matter how mushy things got
otherwise.

Once the case is taken on, is the hero emotionally involved
in the outcome? The Golden Age sleuths cared only about

finding the truth (really about unraveling the puzzle). Gideon of Scotland Yard always cared that the innocent were protected and the guilty brought to justice. But it was a generic caring. Spies rarely care about anything but their own survival and playing the game. Harpur and Iles, in the strong contemporary British police series by Bill James (*Protection, Halo Parade, The Lolita Man, Take*), have a similar attitude—they care about doing the job but more about their own political and sexual survival (in a Bill James book a policeman's lot is a very adulterous one). Maigret was frequently sympathetic with the victim, but sometimes with the killer, and sometimes with the survivors. But not passionately involved. This continues to be true in a lot of books, though it's often masked by a story that puts the hero in danger so he has a desperate concern about staying alive as well as finding the truth.

If the book is going to be an odyssey for the hero, then there must be some relationship between the events in the book and the hero's life. These can be resonances—arousing emotions or issues—or events that happen to the hero, like getting shot or being betrayed or losing his job. There should be situations that test his morality and his ideals. Certainly in my own books each investigation brought the hero's life to a crisis of one sort or another, each story was designed or handled in such a way as to test the limits of his character.

So what should the hero be?

My answer as an adviser to budding writers is that editors would like "a fresh heroine," "with a new and unusual environment," "who gets intimately involved with her cases," and "although he knows better than to tangle with the awesome Criminal Monster, when his beloved aunt Mildred falls victim, he must enter dirty waters" that are "more dangerous than he could possibly know" and "lead to a deadly and fast-paced climax."

My own answer, the one from my heart, is: It's a big hotel, with lots of rooms, and almost anybody can check in. Write it the way you would love to read it.

Next to the paragraph that said, *Heroes and heroines are neither good nor bad in terms of conventional morality. They are good and bad in the terms you—the writer—set in your universe,* my esteemed and excellent editor, Cathy Repetti, wrote, *Not!*—exclamation point and all.

Lots of people would agree with Ms. Repetti.

Author Gallagher Gray was kind enough to write me a three-page letter. All of her opinions disagree with mine and all of them seem to have a certain validity.

> *A hero must possess an inner commitment to imposing fairness and revealing the truth. Otherwise the book would be too much like real life—and what's the point of reading a crime novel if it is just like real life?*

Raymond Chandler wrote in *The Simple Art of Murder*:

> *Down these mean streets a man must go who is himself not mean, who is neither tarnished nor afraid. . . . He must be . . . a man of honor—by instinct, by inevitability, without thought of it, and certainly without saying it. He must be the best man in his world and a good enough man for any world. . . .*

I say:

Chili Palmer (*Get Shorty*, Elmore Leonard): Loan shark, collector, enforcer.

Eddie Coyle (*The Friends of Eddy Coyle*, George V. Higgins): Gun dealer, small-time hoodlum, informant.

Parker (*The Man with the Getaway Face, The Handle, The Sour Lemon Score*, Donald Westlake writing as Richard Stark): Armed robber, cold-blooded killer.

Don Corleone (*The Godfather*, Mario Puzo): Killer; extortionist; major organized crime figure; corrupter of unions, politicians, and judges; runs illegal gambling operations; employs enforcers; orders murders.

Michael Corleone: All of the above, plus he has both his own brother-in-law and his own brother killed.

Harry Morgan (*To Have and Have Not*, Ernest Hemingway): Smuggler, cold-blooded killer, double dealer, racist.

Homeboy (*Homeboy*, Seth Morgan): Junkie, thief, liar, deliberately sets up his best friend to get killed.

Roy Dillon (*The Grifters*, Jim Thompson): Con man with a lust for his mother.

That's not even mentioning the vast assortment of heroes who do incredibly vicious and violent things in the name of justice. Spenser always kills a bunch of people. In *Sharkey's Machine*, by William Diehl, the first time we meet Sharkey he is an undercover cop making a coke buy. He's exposed, the bad guy runs, Sharkey chases him, trading shots in downtown Atlanta during peak shopping hours. Sharkey follows him onto a crowded bus and shoots him there. Three times. Boom! Boom! Bam! In the real world, I don't want this clown on the streets where I live. Or where my mother buys her groceries. Or on the bus that my little girl takes a ride on. Or even in *your* neighborhood. There is no justification for this, even if the dude had been Pablo Escobar, not just a punk peddling zees, which is in fact all the weight the dead dude could handle. But in the world of the thriller, it's cops like Sharkey, street-smart, doing their job, dealing with gutter people by gutter means, who are right and righteous. Deskbound, form-sucking bureaucrats who criticize Sharkey's boundless insanity are cowardly know-nothings and traitors in the war on crime.

My own personal favorite is the heroine of Nancy Taylor Rosenberg's *Mitigating Circumstances*. She's some sort of criminal justice professional, as the jacket copy says Ms. Rosenberg was. A prosecutor, I think. Or probation officer. Anyway, someone breaks into her home and rapes her and her daughter. They report it. She sees a picture of the perpetrator in her photo collection of bad guys, goes to his home, and kills him. Pop!

Then the police bring her daughter to a lineup. Her daughter identifies some other dude, a still-living person, as the perpetrator.

Whoops! Killed the wrong guy. Duh.

Does she suffer paroxysms of guilt like Dostoyevsky's Raskolnikov? Is she even upset? Well, yes, but only about the possibility of being caught.

Is she caught? Well, her best friend, the cop she admires above all others, because he is the most honest cop she's ever met and because he is a man of uncompromised and uncompromising integrity, is getting suspicious. He sniffs out the truth.

What does the cop do about it? Nothin'. Why not? Well, because the guy she killed was a third world, under-class scum bucket who deserved it anyway. For other stuff, but that doesn't matter. He deserved it for *something*. He tells her it's all right, that she done good.

The author has gone to great pains to convince us that he is the man of integrity because he is the device that sets the moral standards by which the heroine's actions can be considered positive, even heroic.

I'm a knee-jerk liberal and I figured this was a great setup for an argument against the sins of vigilantism and for the safeguards of our stodgy old criminal justice system. But no!

It's an "open season on scuzzballs" book. I am appalled by this. So what. Nobody else appears to be. It was marketed as a perfectly normal legal thriller, not an impassioned plea to let every Californian murder at least one person of his or her choice.

The key phrase in Chandler's essay, and the one that stands up to analysis of successful books, is that the hero be "the best man in his world."

The issue is to define the world.

Once again I return to Mario Puzo, who brilliantly turned our normal world inside out. He started with the title. Not *Captain of Crime* or *Capo dei Tutti Capi* or *Biggest Mobster of Them All* or *Gangland King*, but *The Godfather*. Heretofore, the Mafia was a band of criminals in a dreaded secret conspiracy. Now it's a Family. This was so slick a literary event that it forever changed the language of real-life law enforcement. Now even the FBI, which once denied the existence of organized crime, refers fondly to such gangs as "crime families."

The first time we see this Godfather, the first we hear of him, people are lined up outside his door looking for *justice*. The police, the courts, the district attorney, have failed them. All these poor, desperate folk need the assistance, the strength, the support, the moral certitude, of the head of organized crime in New York.

I bought it. Didn't you?

CHAPTER 12

Procedure

This is how I always start:
  "I am the prosecutor.
  "I represent the state. I am here to present to you the evidence of a crime. Together you will weigh the evidence. You will deliberate upon it. You will decide if it proves the defendant's guilt.
  "This man—" And here I point.
                          Scott Turow, *Presumed Innocent*

Procedure is a third and equal partner along with plot and character.

The prototypical mystery novel begin as simply as this: A crime has been committed. It needs to be investigated.

  "He must have died within two or three minutes at most. We'll know more after the autopsy."

> *Maigret looked into the staring eyes [of the corpse].*
> *They were very light blue, or rather a watery gray. The fea-*
> *tures were strongly delineated, especially the powerful*
> *jaw, which was already beginning to sag.*
>
> *The van from Criminal Records drew up at the curb,*
> *and the technicians got out and began unloading their*
> *equipment, for all the world like a film or television cam-*
> *era crew on location.*
>
> *"Have you been in touch with the Department of Pub-*
> *lic Prosecutions?"*
>
> *"Yes. They're sending over a Deputy and Examining*
> *Magistrate."*
>
> Georges Simenon, *Maigret and the Wine Merchant*

There is a subgenre called the police procedural. It used to be a low-key, rather uninflected story about police officers solving crimes in their official and dignified way: television's *Dragnet*; J. J. Marric's series about Scotland Yard (*Gideon's Day, Gideon's Night, Gideon's Week,* etc.); Simenon's eighty or so Maigret novels; and Ed McBain's 87th Precinct novels (*Ghosts, Ice, Mischief*), scruffier and hipper with officers who are more troubled than the old models, but still the body of each book is simply procedure.

Patricia Cornwell's heroine, Dr. Kay Scarpetta (*Postmortem, All That Remains, Body of Evidence*), is a forensic pathologist employed as the chief medical examiner of the state of Virginia. The bulk of what takes place in her books is *procedure*: autopsies, laboratory work, crime scene analysis, evidence collection/preservation/examination, investigative methods, perpetrator and victim profiling, computer analysis, and so on. Each forensic discovery drives the story on to new questions. They, too, will be answered through procedure. This is not to say that there is no plot or action or character. There are all those things, but procedure is the spine of her novels.

It is not character or plot that dictates the march of events in Thomas Harris's novels, *The Silence of the Lambs* and *Red Dragon*; it is procedure. Hair and fiber analysis, bite marks, fingerprints, serial killer and victim profiling, and so on. Will Graham, the hero, is a procedure man, and he tries to connect to the serial killer by figuring out the killer's procedures. How he picks his victims, carries out surveillance, makes his entries, immobilizes the victims.

It is not necessary to be an expert or to have special knowledge to put procedure to the fore. Colin Dexter, the author of the Inspector Morse series, clearly knows little or nothing about police procedure, organization, administration, forensic science, or technology. He's invented his own bumbling amateur methodology for his fictive cop. The bulk of each book is Morse going out and talking to some people, then coming up with a cockamamie theory over a few pints and some classical music, until a new fact emerges that trashes that idea and he does it over again until, like the infinite number of monkeys banging at typewriters for an infinite length of time, the law of averages has him come up with the right theory.

Every investigative novel, with an amateur sleuth or a spy or a Mike Hammer–style pummel-the-answers-out-of-'em PI, has a procedure. The crime is committed. The investigator has to find out whodunit. He applies whatever tools are available to him in logical and unfolding order, each new piece of evidence suggesting the next or an alternative step in procedure.

An excellent tool for writing the next scene is always to ask: If this were real, with what the character knows, with what he is capable of, what could he do next?

The structure of a mystery novel can be viewed as the answer to the question: If this were actually happening, how could the investigator find his way to the heart of the matter?

Or of a spy novel.

Afterwards, in the dusty little corners where London's secret servants drink together, there was argument about where the Dolphin case history should really begin. . . . The hard men . . . they saw the question solely in operational terms. They pointed to Smiley's deft footwork in tracking down Karla's paymaster in Vientiane; to Smiley's handling of the girl's parents; to his wheeling and dealing with the reluctant barons of Whitehall, who held the operational purse strings, and dealt out rights and permissions in the secret world. Above all, to the wonderful moment when he turned the operation round on its own axis. For these pros the Dolphin case was a victory of technique. Nothing more.

John Le Carré, *The Honorable Schoolboy*

Part of what makes the crime novel, the mystery story, the policier, the detective narrative, different is that it is a book about a person with a job to do. A job that matters more than the person. That is as true of the bank robber as it is of the police officer. It is as true of the lawyer as it is of the gangster. The day's assignment, tunneling into the bank, maintaining surveillance, filing a motion, dictates the action. "Character" does not determine what is done, it merely shapes how the actions are carried out. The job itself dispenses consequences; "character" affects only what the reactions to the consequences are.

Sit at your keyboard. Don't think of plot. Think of character only in terms of investigative abilities and limitations. Think of the investigator's position and his resources. Then try to figure out, step by step, what things he can do, and will do, in their logical progression, in their more or less necessary sequence, to figure out whodunit. If you have that, you have a story.

CHAPTER 13

What Is Action?

Action is goal-oriented activity.

Activity without direction is random noise.

There is only one significant difference between quiet action, like speech or thought, and violent action: We *assume* that we do not have to establish that the consequences of violent action are important. Point a gun and you think it's a tension-filled scene because if you fire off fifteen AK-47s and throw a couple of grenades, someone will probably be hurt.

With quiet action you know you have to work at establishing that something is at risk. Done well, there is as much or more tension in watching characters risk humiliation as in watching them risk their lives. As a point of reference I recommend the Horatio Hornblower novels. They're not mysteries, but what the hell, I like them. Although they concern war in wooden ships, an extremely hazardous milieu with a very high mortality rate, the protagonist is far more concerned with how he appears to the world, and to himself, than whether he lives or dies. And we share his concerns.

One of my all-time favorite mystery novels is Josephine Tey's *Daughter of Time*, in which the detective, flat on his back in a hospital bed, investigates the reputation of someone who is five hundred years dead, Richard III (1452–1485). There are no possible contemporary repercussions, no threats to the detective or, for that matter, anyone else. It's not a time travel book in which something that the detective does will save the twins in the tower or change the course of the past. It is simply an investigation, from a hospital bed, with borrowed books, into how that dry and dusty subject, history, is created. It is riveting.

Therefore, looking up sources in old books and getting the answer to a question that doesn't matter to anyone in any material sense is action.

Clarity—in your own mind and on the page—is the first essential for good action. You have to know where everything is, who does what and how, and where it all goes. You have to know what is at stake and establish its value. You have to state it simply and clearly.

I always visualize action as vectors, directions of force, as I was taught to do in Physics 101. Each person and thing has a certain amount of mass, and there is an equation—which I've forgotten—of mass and speed that equals force, and when the various objects in motion crash into each other or into objects at rest, a variety of things happen. Sometimes they start the new object moving, sometimes something breaks, sometimes one or both bounce and go careening in new directions.

Your job is to describe the amount of mass in motion, its speed, its force, and what is expected to happen when it hits. Clearly and simply. The force in motion need not be a fist or a bullet. That's the least of it. It might be the force of history. Or biology. Or grief or lust or rage.

CHAPTER 14

Dialogue

Dialogue is action.

If I say to you, "Raise your hands or I'll shoot you," I have committed an action, whether or not I have a gun. If I say to you, "Your partner has been embezzling money from your company" or "Your husband is sleeping with your brother" or "I saw the shooting. It wasn't Billy, it was Sal," I have committed an action.

All dialogue should be action. Each line of dialogue should be an action. Not necessarily big, not necessarily offensive, possibly defensive, diversionary, delaying, confused, obfuscating, but action nonetheless.

What gives "action" to your dialogue is giving the characters goals (objectives) in each encounter. Sometimes the objective is the explicit subject of the conversation. Often it is not.

There is an acting term, *subtext*, that refers to the thoughts and feelings that are going on below the surface of the dialogue. In the film *Casablanca*, when Rick says, "Play it, Sam. You played it for her, you can play it for me," the line is nothing without the subtext. With the subtext it is one of the most memorable lines in film history.

The objectives of characters are frequently hidden in the subtext.

Clear and graphic examples of subtext are easier to point to in films because there are at least two completely separate delivery systems, the words and the actor. Courtship scenes are almost always played in subtext, which is how it's usually done in life as well. People rarely say, in the words of the Jimmy Buffett song, "Why don't we get drunk and screw?" They suggest it politely with the eyes, body language, and tone of voice, while their words speak of mundane things like buying vegetables or placing a bomb in the bad guy's Lamborghini. Scenes of threat also frequently use subtext, either because it's more stylish or because to utter the threat explicitly is a criminal act.

We book writers don't have actors, but we are likely to have a narrator who can function as the additional delivery system.

This scene is from *Alibi for an Actress*, by Gillian Farrell. Heroine Annie McGrogan is having dinner with her ex-boyfriend. Actors could deliver these lines with the subtext unspoken; the author needs, in this case, to use a narrator.

"So?" I said. Meaning are you ready to explain why you always talked about marriage when I was married and never mentioned it after Patrick and I filed for divorce?

"So," he said, with that mischievous boyish smile that he figured would get him out of having to discuss it.

"So," I said, meaning, no I won't let it slide.

"So," he said, meaning would you like to look at the menu or order a drink first.

"Oh boy," I said, "nothing's changed."

"*Well,*" *he said. He made those love eyes that had se-duced me in the first place.*

"*You still can't talk,*" *I said.*

He signaled for the waiter.

"*You have to say something,*" *I said.* "*I always do all the talking.*"

"*Um,*" *he said.* "*Let's look at the menu. OK?*"

"*Not OK,*" *I said.*

He smiled one of his better smiles and reached across the table to take my hand. My hand tingled. Tears came to my eyes. Again. "*Oh, Rowdy,*" *I sighed. He took his name from the character that Clint Eastwood played on Rawhide. His real name was Gordon. I held my breath. Held it. Held it. He did not speak.*

"*Talk to me, goddamn it,*" *I said.* "*Or I'm walking out of here.*"

"*Annie,*" *he said. Meaning I wish you wouldn't and could you suggest a topic.*

"*Do you even know that you can't talk?*"

"*Annie,*" *he said. Meaning why do you keep after me this way, can't we order?*

"*Do you have any thoughts? Do you have any feelings?*"

"*You look really good tonight,*" *he said.* "*I miss you.*"

"*Do you really?*" *I asked him.*

"*Yes,*" *he said, surrounding the monosyllable with sig-nificance.*

"*Can I express some things to you,*" *I said, wanting to speak of love and involvement and the nature of relation-ships.*

"*Yeah,*" *he said.* "*Sure.*" *Meaning that I could but that he preferred that I wait until we ordered.*

Next is a scene between a man and a wife. He comes home. It's eight at night. She's in the kitchen making bacon and eggs. He's Italian-American. He sells heroin at the middle-man level and he makes a decent living from it. He has just returned from a short stretch in prison. The guy above him on the food chain is his wife's father. This is not an operatic mythological Godfather version of mob life. They live in an OK suburban house in New Jersey. Nikki, the wife, has a job in the city, at a bank, calling people who are behind on their credit cards and trying to get them to pay. While her husband was in prison she met a young Puerto Rican lawyer and had an affair with him. She thinks her lover looks like a movie star. She also thinks of him as a nigger, though his hair is straight.

> "I'd figured I'd find you here," he said.
> "Why?"
> "Because you don't stay out shopping last three weeks."
> "So that's why you decided to come home?"
> "I don't know."
> "Make you something to eat?"
> "No. I got to meet some people later."
> "Then why did you bother to come home?"
> "I don't know. I figured you'd be here."
> "Well, I am."
> She took the bacon and eggs on a tray and went out and sat on the couch and watched television as she ate. She sat on the end of the couch nearest the window. Her husband sat on the opposite end. Both studied the television. . . .
> "If it's that job that's bothering you, and I'm betting it's that freakin' job, I told you to quit."
> "It's not the job."
> They sat in silence and pretended to watch television.
> "Well, if it isn't the job, then it's something else," he said.

"*It is.*"

"*What?*"

"*Something died when you were in jail. I don't know how to explain it, but something died.*"

"*Is there some other guy?*" *He asked it calmly, but she knew . . . an affirmative answer would have produced immediate murder.*

"*No,*" *she said.*

"*Do you love me,*" *he said.*

She wanted to tell him she loved him for the past, for her family, for her way of life, but not as a husband is loved. Instead, staring straight ahead, she just said, "Yes."

"*Then we need time,*" *her husband said.*

"*I don't know,*" *she said.*

Jimmy Breslin, *Forsaking All Others*

Sometimes the objectives are completely invisible. When the client hires the detective to do a job, but the job isn't really what they say it is, the subtext should be undetectable, to the detective as well as to the reader. But you know, and the character in the scene who is lying knows, and that will make a difference.

Invisible objectives can still animate a scene.

Personally, once I have decided on the two main factors in the scene—what the characters want to achieve and what I need to achieve—then I find dialogue scenes are the easiest scenes to write. This is when I actually do have the feeling of scenes "writing themselves." I usually have some notes that mention some of the plot things that need to be covered in the scene, possibly some theme things, plus any gags or shticks or setups or set pieces, and these act both as prompts to keep the scene going and guides to keep it from wandering too far off course. But basically I have the two characters in my head, or on the page, or in my voice, going at it from their own points of view, and it just rolls along and it fills up the pages, and that is very satisfying.

To some degree I speak aloud, or simulate speaking aloud to my inner ear, while I write dialogue. I talk with accents, attitudes, pauses, and all that other stuff.

To check it, I read aloud. Actually I read everything aloud to check it, but dialogue in particular.

> *You will find, to your delight, that reading your own work aloud, even silently, is the most astonishingly easy and reliable method that there is for achieving economy in prose, efficiency of description, and narrative effect as well. . . . Rely upon it: if you can read it aloud to yourself without wincing, you have probably gotten it right.*
> George V. Higgins, *On Writing: Advice for Those Who Write to Publish (Or Would Like To)*

Reading aloud should instantly tell you if your dialogue is wooden or alive, speakable or unspeakable, appropriate to the characters, inappropriate, or just generic. If you have doubts, tape-record it and listen to the tape recordings. If you cringe when you hear it, great, you had the opportunity to cringe before your deathly prose was set in stone, put on a page, and placed in the bookstore, at which time you would have to cringe over exposing your fault publicly. That's why God put erasers on computers.

SOME NOTES ABOUT DIALOGUE

Real speech is nonlinear. A lot of dialogue in books, especially mysteries, detective novels, techno-thrillers, and so on, is expository and must be expository, and this naturally creates a tendency to writing stiff, formal, unnatural talking that isn't speech at all but exposition with quotation marks slapped on it, he saids and she saids inserted in the odd openings.

Spend some time listening to conversations among your friends. Listen to your own. Real speech is only linear and organized and coherent and in complete sentences and paragraphs when it is prescripted. A politician's speech, an attorney's summation, a sales pitch, are some examples.

Yet completely real speech is too wandering, elusive, and tedious to reproduce in an unremitting way on the page.

So for the most part I would say that the goal is a form of speech that has all the benefits of organized thought and rewrites and art and style and wit and other good stuff, but that has enough of the tics and characteristics of natural speech that the reader can feel he's hearing something close to real.

So—a couple of tricks:

1. Give your characters subgoals in their scenes. Hunger, thirst, a desire to show off, to entice, to share their feelings for art, to find a cure for hemorrhoids. Let the subgoals play into and out of the main dialogue.

2. Don't put exposition or long summaries into dialogue unless there is a dialogue reason to do so, and then only to the degree that dialogue reasons require you to.

   What are dialogue reasons? Dialogue shows character. Dialogue is a form of action; exposition, for the most part, is not. Dialogue permits characters to lie. To be wrong. To misunderstand. To reveal less than the whole truth or embellish. To color, to minimize, to manipulate. Dialogue permits certain kinds of wit, pathos, bathos, humor, threat, despair, that exposition does not. So if the scene is going to show one of those things, do it in dialogue. If not, feel free to break away from the dialogue and sum-

marize. If you have a character explain the international
monetary fund for no other reason than for us, the readers, to understand the IMF, just say—"She told Detective
Inspector McGorgle how the IMF worked. It is an organization of . . ."

3. Get out when it's time to get out. I sometimes find myself
stuck in the construction I've chosen for a scene. If it's in
dialogue, I feel I have to stay with the dialogue. If the detective is receiving information in dialogue form, I have
trouble breaking away from it into narrator summary
form. This is silly. I can do it if I want to. Of course, the
reverse is true. I can season summary with choice bits of
dialogue. A similar thing happens with scenes. I start one
and I can't get out or get to the end. There's a certain
level at which you put on your Nikes and "just do it."
Your characters are not on a stage where you must walk
them in and out, they're in a movie—CUT. FADE TO BLACK.
DISSOLVE. CUT TO:

HE HISSED, SHE MOANED.
SOME MORE NOTES ABOUT DIALOGUE

Reviewers love to nail writers for "he hissed." They suddenly get literal and precise and count the sibilants in the
sentence that was supposedly hissed and take stupendous
satisfaction in hissing that one can't hiss without esses.
Moaned, barked, howled, cried, panted, snorted, huffed,
yelped, shrieked, heaved, growled, purred, are also like
leading with your chin. We're in a minimalist period. I'm
not sure why. "He said," "she said," seem to be all that a
writer is supposed to tell the reader in any given line of dialogue. George Higgins can actually get through an entire
book with no more than "Cogan said" and "Frankie said."

Most people will slip in "asked," "replied," "went on," "continued." Those are neutral, so they're also OK.

The current fashion is to not overdirect the actors who speak the lines in the readers' heads but to leave them some latitude to create their own phrasing.

But the lines of dialogue with just "he said," "she said," can't possibly convey what most writers want to communicate the way they want to communicate. Here are some approaches.

"Sure." Kathy nodded, as if settling an argument with herself that Dante was not privy to. "But if you get hurt in there, I'll kill you," throwing him a faint courteous smile.

Bob Leuci, *Fence Jumpers*

A kid's sigh. "Okay, all right, ask me."
Bud, soft. "Cindy said Duke told her to look after you if something happened to him. Do you think he figured something was going to happen?"

James Ellroy, *L.A. Confidential*

"Well, you're wrong," Bart said triumphantly. "That was the day of George Millace's funeral and Elgin sent me a cable . . ." He hesitated and his eyes flickered, but he went on, " . . . and the cable came from Hong Kong."
"A cable of regrets, was it?"
"George Millace," Bart said with venom, "was a shit."

Dick Francis, *Reflex*

"There aren't facts," said Peter Worthington, thoroughly irritated again.

John Le Carré, *The Honorable Schoolboy*

Yes, then there's John Le Carré, who is full of "Connie prompted brightly," "Connie inquired, all interest," "Doris reminded him eventually," "Sam asked, very leisurely," "Guillam snapped," "said Martello heartily, in his warm, confiding voice," "growled Sol the veteran, in a voice as dry as his hand," "she murmured," "Tui remarked handsomely," "the girl cried angrily," "Di Salis chimed"—and that doesn't seem to bother anyone at all.

CHAPTER 15

Details &
Descriptions

What are significant details and how should you describe them?

A significant detail is something that has push or is a symbol of push. By push I mean possessing a force that drives a person.

To be sure, the grass was very dry, and one ember could easily have the low hills of grazing swept black in minutes. A bleak, blond land, with scattered thorn bush making smudges of dull green like white women's eyeshadow, and bare patches of earth the pinky red of their sunburn. A hard land, too, that gave nothing for nothing. A good place for puff adders and lizards and the shrikes that hung their prey on the barbed-wire fences.

His watch had stopped and the car had no radio. But judging by the sun, it was still before eight. Plenty of time

to smoke a Stuyvesant and take another look at the map.
At least the car, a beaten-up Anglia, had much that was
useful in it.

Zondi had about another ten kilometers. . . .

He was thankful not to be in a hurry once the corruga-
tions of the dirt road, regular as those in washboard, began to drum beneath four very doubtful tires. There were
also potholes big enough to swallow a wheel and sharp
stones that clattered like hail on the car's underside. The
dust, however, was the worst of the lot. . . . He was glad to
be in a car and not, as long ago, on the seat of a donkey
cart beside his father. Then the stones had been the worst
as passing vehicles shotgunned them up at you. Once he
had been hit on the ear—which was better luck than the
donkey had met on another occasion, when it lost an eye.

James McClure, *The Gooseberry Fool*

The place is South Africa during apartheid, where even the
landscape is infected with metaphors of race. Zondi is a cop.
But a black one, a Bantu. Note the distinctly second-class car.
The story, although it is relatively low-key, distinctly realistic,
straight forward policier, is permeated with race, the politics
of race, and with what it means to live in that land.

Where you were born pushes you. To be born in Johannes-
burg will make you a different person than if you are born in
Brooklyn. To be born in 1945 is to be different than to be
born in 1975. Class, race, time, and place. Gender, parent-
age, education. The weather, your insulation from the
weather, your economic condition, your equipment, your car
and your clothes, the food you eat, where and how you eat it.
Moments of embarrassment, hope of praise, the level of activity in your glands, what you think beauty is, and what
brings esteem among your people. These are forces that

move a person in a certain direction. Vectors. They can be drawn on a blackboard.

Force creates motion. Motion is action. Out of actions come drama.

The events in the story determine what details you should give the reader. If they are details that affect how the characters are going to act or that are symbolic of how the characters are apt to act, then they have a certain life to them; they're like latent verbs.

According to my passport my name is Richard Cochrane. That's not true. My native home is Ireland. That's not true either. I'm an exile, an expatriate, a man without a country, a stateless person. Here in a white land. A snow-covered alpine country where they speak a language I barely understand in a landscape like none I've ever known.

But who cares. I have money in the bank. They have excellent banks here. But they do almost everywhere these days. I have a full-breasted young woman as my companion. Younger than me. Heavy breasted, round bellied, and ripe with child. My child. She says so. I believe her. Her passport says her name is Marie. That's true. Marie Laure. My passport says my profession is priest. That's not true. On the one recent occasion that anyone has actually read the slot by profession and looked at Marie's belly at the same time, I just grinned. The border guard grinned back. He was happier with the notion of a lecherous priest than of a false passport. The image harked back to a merrier age—Chaucerian, Machiavellian, Rabelaisian—when priests and even politicians were presumed to have penises. The alternative, the modern reality of false papers, would have just meant more work.

This is another description of the same character:

I am 5 feet 11 inches and weigh one hundred and seventy-two pounds. My eyes are a deep rich canine brown, my hair is a dark brown, dark enough that it looks black in bad light. I keep it cut to a moderate length. Not so short as to look like a recruit, not so long as to look Bohemian. And it parts on the left. I have some scar tissue over my left eye where the skin was split against the bone. You have to look close to see it because it is, for the most part, under the eyebrow. Also the shape of my nose has been altered somewhat by being broken when I was twenty years or so younger. The air is thin up here, my skin tans easily so my face is very dark. It's a winter tan so that when I take off my shirt everything from the neck down looks quite white in comparison even though my essential complexion is Mediterranean. I ski a lot and that makes my legs strong and fit but my muscles are not sculpted like someone who goes to the health club and uses the machines. My favorite color in clothing is blue, dark blue and I normally wear jeans and a ski jacket. I have three different ski jackets. I prefer shells with attachable or fold-up hoods with separate liners. The weather in the mountains is rapidly variable.

I live in an Austrian ski resort named St. Anton in a region called the Arlberg. I have a girlfriend.

Both these passages describe the main character in *Foreign Exchange*. They're both about the same length. If you thought the second one was better than the first, I'm in big trouble. The first is from the book, the second is meant to be an example of bad writing.

Nothing's actually happening in the first passage, but it's

dynamic with possibility. The man who is speaking is in a very dangerous situation—living on a fake passport. He can't go home for reasons unknown. He's in love, he's happy, he's merry, and he's a fool. Anybody can see through him, including dumb-ass border guards. He's just been lucky that no one gives a damn—yet. They will. There's a baby coming, too. That's also going to bring big changes, make his blithe life take a major turn to the serious—and he doesn't seem to have a clue.

It isn't what you write about that matters, it's whether it matters to the characters and the story. All sorts of tedious historical trivia, pastoral tediums, doilies, interior decorations, flower arrangements, any damn thing at all—so long as they can push people into stealing or lying or committing adultery or killing. Then they are alive.

I was wearing my powder-blue suit, with dark blue shirt, tie and display handkerchief, black brogues, black wool socks with dark blue clocks on them. I was neat, clean, shaved and sober, and I didn't care who knew it. I was everything the well-dressed private detective ought to be. I was calling on four million dollars.

The main hallway of the Sternwood place was two stories high. Over the entrance doors, which would have let in a troop of Indian elephants, there was a broad stained-glass panel showing a knight in dark armor rescuing a lady who was tied to a tree and didn't have any clothes on but some very long and convenient hair. The knight had pushed the visor of his helmet back to be sociable, and he was fiddling with the knots of the ropes that tied the lady to the tree and not getting anywhere. I stood there and thought that if I lived in the house, I would sooner or later have to climb up there and help him. He didn't seem to be really trying.

There were French doors at the back of the hall, behind them a wide sweep of emerald grass to a white garage, in front of which a slim dark young chauffeur in shiny black leggings was dusting a maroon Packard convertible. Beyond the garage were some decorative trees trimmed as carefully as poodle dogs.

That's from the opening of *The Big Sleep* (1939), by Raymond Chandler. It is a fairly straightforward descriptive passage. It's quite similar to many others, especially many others since. Yet it continues to work. Why?

For starters, it contains real specificity: "black wool socks with dark blue clocks on them." (The hidden rhythm and rhyme aren't so bad either.) Some unobtrusively startling images: "powder-blue suit, with dark blue shirt." Visualize that for a moment and think about what it says about the man wearing it, wearing it in this place, and telling you he's a "well-dressed private detective."

Then there's the place. It speaks not only of money but of a certain kind of spending—lavish, stylish, ostentatious, and imitation Old World. The stained-glass window is good as a status symbol but also as a symbol of the story that's about to come. Marlowe's reaction to it gives it even more resonance: it's got attitude, he's got attitude—it could be a meaningful relationship.

"Emerald grass . . . white garage . . . slim dark young chauffeur in shiny black leggings . . . dusting a maroon Packard convertible." The house and grounds is a place that's as vivid and stylized as a movie set. And even without knowing the story you feel that something is going to happen with that "slim dark young chauffeur."

Books used to have a lot more description than they do now. Before television, before motion pictures, before photo magazines, before photography, before pictures in newspapers, before reproduction technology even of drawings—

there was the word, and the word was used to paint pictures. Of Chinamen and dragons and sea storms and the inside of palaces and the faces of dead saints. Of jungles and tundra and heaven and hell. And those words were used to describe those things to people who had never seen them. But now everybody's seen everything. Read Dickens, or Wilkie Collins, and see how long and tedious the descriptions seem. Lary Crews, who also made this observation, used the example of a kangaroo. There was a time when the writer would have had to assume that his readers did not know what a kangaroo looked like. Imagine the time and space you need to explain what a kangaroo is. You won't do that in your book. You'll just say: " . . . and there was a kangaroo sitting on the sofa."

The media has given us a whole vocabulary of shorthand references. When we describe a car, for the most part we don't describe it. We use a brand name. And maybe one or two hot details.

> *James Bond had been nursing his car, the old Continental Bentley—the 'R' type chassis with the big 6 engine and a 13:40 back axle ratio—that he had now been driving for three years, along that fast but dull stretch of N.1 between Abbeville and Montreuil.*
>
> *. . . Triple wind-horns screamed their banshee discord in his ear, and a low, white two-seater, a Lancia Flaminia Zagato Spyder with its hood down, tore past him, cut in cheekily across his bonnet and pulled away, the sexy boom of its twin exhausts echoing back from the border of the trees. And it was a girl driving, a girl with a shocking pink scarf tied round her hair.*
>
> Ian Fleming, *On Her Majesty's Secret Service*

The whole Bond mythology lives in this little bit.

I love the Lancia Flaminia Zagato Spyder. I don't know if

Fleming invented the use of name brands as an essential literary tool, but he is clearly one of its pioneers, and his books are certainly where I learned it from.

Brand names do a lot: they characterize (we are what we buy), they give the book and the author an air of knowledgeability (this is what the "in" crowd uses or, à la Tom Clancy, this is the very latest thing in air-to-air missiles), and they give verisimilitude to the most transparent fantasy.

Sex, peer pressure, self-image, history, economics, drug use, education, trauma, finance, money, heart rate, disease, social customs, fear of embarrassment, the need for admiration, fear of death, moods, disposition—are all forces that cause behavior.

Food, furniture, clothing, cars, manner of speech, accent, hairstyle, carriage, habitual facial cast and momentary expressions, position in relation to other people, taste in music—are all symbols of character and class; they indicate underlying feelings, drives, attitudes toward life.

You can approach each character—and also each scene—if you are a methodical person who preplans, and make a list of the forces that shape the person's behavior both in general and in the specific action in the upcoming scene, then make a list of those things that might illuminate them.

Or, more likely, you will describe people and scenes as those descriptions occur to you, and then when you go back and reread and certain scenes are flat and certain passages are boring and others seem to be lacking, you can subject them to analysis. Does the information I have given the reader move the story? Is it emblematic or symptomatic or symbolic of the forces that move the characters? Do I fail to tell the readers the things they should know about the time, the place, the people?

This is the first appearance of one of the main characters in *American Hero*.

Then Maggie Krebs walks in. Maggie is one of the ten most beautiful women in the world. That's official. Right out of People magazine. You know her as Magdalena Lazlo, movie star. I know her as Maggie Krebs, divorcée. I helped her get that divorce and keep her fortune. Maggie was always attached to her money, but aren't we all.

Having that much high-powered glamour walk into our drab offices is not unique, but it is unusual. A lot of stars—you see them around if you've ever worked The Strip or the Hollywood beat—are products of their handlers, make-up people and hairdressers, wardrobe and plastic surgeons. Products of our imagination in a way. But even off screen and dressed down, Maggie has it. Everybody watched her, men and women, when she came down to my office.

"Hi ya, Joe," she says. She looks me direct in the eye, gives me that smile, and that voice—you can read anything you want to into that voice—just the way she talked in Highway To Hell—and boom, you could knock me over with a toothpick. I don't let it show, but I figure she knows what that "Hi ya, Joe," can do. How can she not know? It's her business, making strong men weak and weak men strong.

What I think is interesting about this is that, in a sense, there is no description. It doesn't mention Maggie's hair color or hairstyle, eye color, height, weight, age, accent, wardrobe, the shape of her face, the type of figure she has. Joe does describe her one more time:

I don't have to describe her in detail. You've seen her on screen. If you haven't, go rent a cassette. The vibrancy, they say, comes across on film—the curve of her back, how long her legs are—remember that long pan up her legs, seemed to take forever, when she played a call girl in that Burt Reynolds film—the shape of her breasts, even the texture of her nipples when they're erect—the full screen CU of one of them, and it really is her, she didn't use a tit double, in White Lady—*so you know what it is I'm looking at.*

No one's ever told me that they noticed that she is never described. At least one person told me how vivid my portrait of her was and how they could see her. Several people have described her to me as a blonde. Others as a brunette. People who are Hollywood savvy have told me they know which movie star she's modeled on.

CHAPTER 16

Subject Matter

THE APPEAL OF INFORMATION

Forensic pathology has put Patricia Cornwell on the best-seller list. Michael Crichton essentially writes dramatized essays on scientific *(Andromeda Strain, Jurassic Park, Congo)*, social *(Rising Sun)*, and historical situations *(The Great Train Robbery)*. *Presumed Innocent,* the first big post–Perry Mason legal thriller, was a gritty tour of how criminal law is really practiced. Joseph Wambaugh, earlier, did the same thing for the police novel and was the first to give us a real insider's view of what being a cop is like. Tom Clancy, although an amateur, knows more, and told more, about modern military technology than anyone else ever had in thriller form. Actually, I wouldn't be surprised if Ronald Reagan got more out of reading Clancy than he did out of Pentagon briefings, which says something about all three of them and is meant as a compliment to Clancy.

Clancy and Wambaugh and Turow had so much impact that they each, with a single book, created subgenres, the techno-thriller, the cop novel, and the legal thriller.

WHAT SUBJECT?

Pick subject matter that interests you enough for you to live with it for twelve to sixty months. Or, if you're thinking about a series, maybe a lifetime.

Aside from that, the choice of subject matter is irrelevant. You can make a book about anything that you can stick with long enough to do it.

"High concept," a Hollywood term, refers to a work centered around a powerful idea that can be expressed in a single simple sentence. A short one. You see it very frequently in so-called breakout novels and very hot first novels. Grisham's *The Firm*, Turow's *Presumed Innocent*, Wambaugh's *The New Centurions*, all have a high concept quality to them. All of Michael Crichton's immensely successful books are high concept novels.

Romans à clef (representations of actual events and real persons in the guise of fiction) and pseudo romans à clef, especially about celebrities, have market power. General fiction is littered with live and dead Kennedys and Monroes. There's less of it in crime fiction.

Subjects—sometimes—help publishers. A publisher has two real questions about a book: Can I sell it? How can I sell it?

If the answer is "I can sell it as a legal thriller. The Grisham and Turow buyers, having read all the Grishams and Turows, will buy it," that's good. So is "Ah, a serial killer novel, we can sell it as another *Silence of the Lambs*."

If it's about Northern Ireland, you might hear, "Northern Ireland books don't sell." Which doesn't mean it's true, or that your book about The Troubles won't.

But these are murky waters indeed. Second-guessing publishers is not as awful as second-guessing producers or the American voter, but it's not an entirely rational exercise. And it's probably tough enough to do all the other stuff without figuring what subject matter they'll think they'll know how to sell a year or two from the moment you sit down to start.

DO I NEED A SUBJECT?

No.

Dashiell Hammett, Raymond Chandler, Ross Macdonald, Agatha Christie, Ellery Queen, P. D. James, George Higgins, Patricia Highsmith, Sue Grafton, cannot be said to have subjects. Certainly not in the sense that Michael Crichton or Gerald Seymour or Eric Ambler do.

I firmly believe that it's not what you do, it's how you do it. There have been lots of Mafia novels but only one *The Godfather*. Other people have horse-racing mysteries; there's only one Dick Francis. There are several "medieval" mysteries; there's only one *Name of the Rose*. There are lots of serial killer books; none have done as well as Thomas Harris's. There are uncounted legal thrillers. They stand in serried rows behind Grisham and Turow.

WRITE ABOUT WHAT YOU KNOW

Interesting idea.

Certainly setting a book in a milieu with which you are familiar—your hometown, high school or college, your day job—is a lot less work, and that work will be a lot less prone to error, than a book set in a place or time you've never been to.

There's an American writer who sets her books in Great Britain. English people tell me they're horribly inaccurate. She's regularly on the bestseller lists in the U.S.A. Lots of people write cop novels who don't know cops and don't want to know them. Some of them are bestsellers.

I started *Foreign Exchange* with the intention of writing a techno-thriller. Quite frankly, I was hoping to hitch a ride on the bandwagon. I found that I could not master the material. So I worked out the situation in human and political terms, areas with which I was more comfortable.

I attempted to write a novel set in an area like my home in Ulster County, New York. I did research by getting a job on my local paper. I worked very hard. But I couldn't make a book happen. The things I had learned about local personalities and politics were so specific that I got stuck in them. I couldn't get the characters to do things for my story. They had their own lives. Then, on a trip to Germany, I got into a conversation about Brecht and Kafka, both of whom had written about America without ever having been there. Their vision came from a gaudy, tawdry motion picture muse. This was a liberating concept. I decided to write a book about war and Hollywood, places I had never been but only knew through images. *American Hero* has been, to the time of this writing, my most successful book.

Write what you're comfortable writing about would be a better rule of thumb. If it's unknown and you can research your way in, that's fine. If you're comfortable writing about things you know nothing about, and if you can do it in a convincing or charming or entertaining way so that, for the most part, your ignorance doesn't bother anyone, that's also fine.

Subject matter and entertainment through education are not a necessity. It is an option. It can be a powerful one.

CHAPTER 17

Research & Details

I love research. What's exciting about research are the things you learn that you weren't looking for. Finding what you were looking for is about as thrilling as checking your spelling with a dictionary. The more you search, the more unexpected treasure you kick over and the richer and more fun your work gets.

There are lots of ways and places to do research. If you're somewhat shy like I am, you'll prefer the library. If you're more gregarious and aggressive, you may go more for personal interviews and observation and hanging out. That's better, because while you're gathering information, you also have the opportunity to meet characters and appropriate their lines and looks and mannerisms, even their very souls, and use them in your books.

If the mystery is to be more than a puzzle machine or vicarious machismo maker, then it must deal with substance.

Tom Wolfe in his introduction to *The New Journalism*—which is about the novel as much or more than it is about journalism—speaks eloquently about realism, which is not about stolid, prosaic restrictions on style. It is about getting content out of the real world and getting that content right. "The introduction of realism into literature by people like Richardson, Fielding and Smollett was like the introduction of electricity into machine technology. It was not just another device. It raised the state of the art to a new magnitude." And the route to this content is research. "Novelists routinely accepted the unpleasant task of doing reporting, legwork, 'digging,' in order to *get it just right*. That was part of the process of writing novels. Dickens traveled to three towns in Yorkshire using a false name and pretending to be looking for a school . . . in order to get inside the notorious Yorkshire boarding schools to gather material for *Nicholas Nickleby*."

> *I generally suggest nonfiction . . . as a model for the fiction writer chiefly because I think it makes an important point dramatically:* You cannot write well without data. . . .
>
> *The best writing school in the world, in my estimation, is the one that has branches in every major city on the globe; it's called the Associated Press. . . .*
>
> *Solid reportage is interesting precisely because the reporter has gone to the trouble of acquiring information about his or her subject, and then has carefully organized it, so that the reader completing the text knows something that he or she did not know before.*
>
> George V. Higgins, *On Writing: Advice for Those Who Write to Publish (Or Would Like To)*

Certainly some of the very best crime writing in the last thirty years comes from writers who were considered "New

Journalists"; Jimmy Breslin (*The Gang That Couldn't Shoot Straight, Forsaking All Others, World Without End, Amen*), Hunter S. Thompson (*Hell's Angels*), Truman Capote (*In Cold Blood*), Peter Maas (*Serpico, The Valachi Papers, Manhunt, In a Child's Name*), Joe McGinniss (*Fatal Vision*), and Bob Daley (*Prince of the City, Target Blue, Man With a Gun, Year of the Dragon*). Many of these are more than just good books, they are books that actually changed the way we look at writing and the way we think about crime.

The crime novel, unlike the literary novel, never abandoned realism. That is part of its strength and one of the reasons for its survival. But that's an aside. The point is that research is a very powerful tool. It can be hard and daunting work. Peter Blauner spent six months as a volunteer in a New York City Probation Department office to research *Slow Motion Riot*. Richard Price spent months on the streets and in the housing projects to write *Clockers*. The further you go with it, the more you will bring back.

In first novels, even in the first several novels, this may not be too important if you've picked a story for which you can draw on the life you've already lived and its accidental research. Clearly the cop who becomes a novelist has done a ton of accidental research. He's loaded with it. As has someone who's worked in a forensic pathologist's laboratory or in a state prosecutor's office. But any place you've worked, a bank, a ship, a brokerage house—even a video store, like Quentin Tarantino—can provide enough material for at least one book. Maybe three or four or five. But several books down the line, it may be many, it may be few, the well begins to run dry. Directed research may be the answer at that point.

After four straightforward mysteries Justin Scott had an idea for a breakthrough thriller. A supertanker runs down a pleasure boat. Casually, inadvertently. The captain and crew aren't even aware that it happened. They sail on without stopping. There are two people on the boat, husband and wife. The wife dies. The husband vows revenge. It's a story about ships and sailing. Subjects that Justin knew very little about. He researched the book for a year. He booked passage on a ten-thousand-ton Polish freighter from Cape Fear, North Carolina, to Rotterdam, spending most of the time on the bridge. From there he went to England and toured a supertanker and sailed with the pilots from port out to sea, though it took him three months to get permission. He found a boat that would be just like the sailboat in the book, got the specs, and spoke to people who had actually sailed her. He sailed with a knowledgeable, articulate yachtsman and asked a million questions and read a dozen accounts of offshore sailing. The result was a book that appeared to have been written by a sailor who used a lifetime of background as grist for his mill. *Ship Killer* was a bestseller.

This is *a* way. Not *the* way. Not even the most successful way. There are very successful writers who do little or no research. If you can write your books without research, you will write them faster. If research will not improve your books in a way that will make them sell more, then research is a waste of time, adversely affecting your earnings-to-effort ratio.

There are also writers who adamantly disbelieve in realism and in the appeal of realism. Some of them are quite successful.

DETAILS

A few years ago I got a letter postmarked Verbier, Switzerland. Although the writer liked my book *Foreign Exchange*, he pointed out that I had misspelled Valluga, a mountain peak in Austria; Courchevel appeared as Courcheval; and I called Dick's Tea Bar, a club in Val-d'Isère, Dick's T-Bar. People notice. Worse, to get the details wrong is to shatter credibility, lose the suspension of disbelief and the trust of the reader. If I don't know that Dick's T-bar is Dick's Tea Bar, why should the reader who knows skiing trust me about the other things in the book—Japanese industrial spies, the fall of the Soviet-bloc, and relationships between men and women?

Details must be correct. They must be checked. You will get some help from the copy editor and the proofreader. But stuff like Valluga and Dick's Tea Bar will often be up to you.

As a reader, I find that sort of detail always very important, and I was quick to nail a writer who got it wrong and reject his book because he said traffic on Forty-fifth Street in Manhattan runs west to east when I knew it ran the other way. I didn't want to read a book by someone who knew less than I did. When I wrote my first book I would get terribly hung up on those details and my writing would come to a crashing halt until I found out what was on the menu at Lanza's or what TV show would have been playing on NBC at 8:00 P.M. in 1968. I was right to care. I was wrong to let it stop me in my tracks.

You may have noticed that I have a tendency to make a clear and unequivocal statement and then point out the opposite point of view or offer contradictory evidence. I wrote back to the guy from Verbier. We ended becoming very good friends and he arranged for me to have several weeks of the best skiing in my life.

Detail Trick #1: Slug it

Don't take too much time over noncritical details during the first draft. If you're not sure how many stories there are in the Empire State Building and you have no quick and easy way to check and it does not vitally affect the plot, take your best guess, then note it and the page number in a file called "things to check." If you simply don't know something—as opposed to not being sure if what you know is correct—slug it. Write, "He was staying at the XXXX Hotel, a bastion of prewar luxury." If these items survive the second and third draft—then check them.

Detail Trick #2: Evasion

You know you don't know everything. You can't. That awareness may keep you from tackling the many subjects that will bring you to the abyss of your gigantic ignorance. It can cripple your will and make you a wallflower at the dance of prose.

If you can't find out, try writing around it. Writing around stuff is really important and an important thing to learn to do.

Detail Trick #3: Take a chance

Write it wrong if you have to. Then get readers, especially specialists, to read your next-to-last draft. They will spot things and, if you're lucky, tell you how to correct them. A public defender and a police officer who read the manuscript of *You Get What You Pay For* both noted that I had a guy doing time in a state prison on a federal rap, But "ten years for using an interstate telephone to commit a felonious conspiracy" was too good to let go of. I was also in love with the sound of Dannemora, the state prison, and with its location, "between nowhere, nowhere, and Canada." So I made the crime a parole violation, and Santino "The Wrecker" Scorcese was facing a federal sentence after he completed his state time. I sent *Foreign Exchange* to Lito Tejada Flores, who writes brilliantly about skiing, to tell me if I got the ski stuff wrong. He corrected my French and my description of hoarfrost. Marine Lt. Col. (Ret.) Ky L. Thompson corrected several very notable errors I'd made in *American Hero* about military matters.

Themes

Explain how this passage from Hamlet *by William Shake-speare illustrates the major themes.*

—from any high school English exam

This theme stuff is probably very damaging for young writ-ers, and I don't know if it's any good for readers, young or old, either. It's ass-backward. Books aren't themes. They are specifics. Themes are vast, soft, gooey generalities. Books are concrete details. If you try to write themes, you will write pretentious, vague, nebulous, cumulous nimbuses. Fat clouds.

Lary Crews has a line about description, that it should be "a slave, not a master." So it should be, must be, with themes.

Themes should be tools.

If, for example, I were to write a book about a dishonest

public official, then corruption could well be my theme. As I designed my characters, however I sketched them out, I might ask myself, "In what way is this person compromised?" and "In what situation would this character become corrupt? Or not become corrupt?" This would, potentially, add a dimension. It would give me a focal point around which to design my incidents. But not all the incidents. Some of them.

It can be a powerful tool.

Identifying the theme was a key ingredient in writing Gillian Farrell's first book, *Alibi for an Actress*. As was mentioned in the chapter on character, Gillian's life as an actress-detective had been developed as a script. It didn't work, largely, she felt, because it had picked up on the wrong theme. It had been about detecting. Her story was about acting. So she had to come up with a plot and additional characters that would focus on acting.

It's worth noting she had a group of strong characters, from life, outside the acting world, and it kept things from getting claustrophobic.

American Hero was conceived of as a book about the Gulf War as a made-for-TV movie. That's a notion that has several themes inherent in it: the nature of war; the nature of war as seen through the media; the nature of illusion. This last affected how I wrote about sex and about relationships. It made them different than they would have been if the themes had been different.

You can let the themes color the characters. You can use the themes to suggest facets of the characters that you display. The themes may prompt you to invent incidents or to shape incidents or to add details. But you can't write the themes. You must write incidents, characters, and details.

CHAPTER 19

First Person, Third Person

Narrative voice, the "who" who is speaking to the reader, is usually divided into first person ("I was sitting at my bullet-proof desk, feeling not at all investigatory, when . . .") and third person ("George was really feeling despair of a particularly carnal order, but Sally, in her obstinacy, could only sense his kindness"). The third person is usually assumed to be the voice of God, omniscient and omnipresent. But if you look at what writers actually do, there's a real sliding scale of narrative voices:

First person with an occasional third-person scene (usually, but not always, just one, and that one being the first).

First person disguised as third person: That's when the narrator writes about everything in the third person, but no scene takes place without the hero being present. The narrator and the hero have identical attitudes and the narrator can see inside only one mind, the hero's. All others are as they would appear in the first-person narrative. Alan Dershowitz wrote his lawyer novel, *The Advocate's Devil*, in this voice.

Second person: That's Dr. Watson, the sidekick, who narrates the hero's adventures.

Team Third Person: I know only one author who does this, John Le Carré. There are probably more. In the Smiley trilogy, *Tinker Tailor Soldier Spy*, *The Honorable Schoolboy*, and *Smiley's People*, the narrator's voice is that of an in-house historian, or of a very personal debriefer, someone who has had in-depth interviews with a number of the participants. Each scene has the debriefer's overview but also features one person, and the scene is primarily from that one person's view, and during that scene we are privy to only that one person's thoughts. If that person shows up in another scene that happens to "belong" to someone else, we won't hear his thoughts. The people whose thoughts we can share are limited to people on Smiley's team—never one of the opposition.

Alternating Persons: One scene, one person. All sides. Very useful for contest plots.

Third Person: We see into every person's heart as the spirit moves the narrator, or as the plot demands. Some examples are Jimmy Breslin's *Forsaking All Others* and Bob Leuci's *Fence Jumpers*.

The Camera: We see into no one's heart. We see only what is done. We hear only what is said. In addition, or in subtraction, there is no history, no sociology, no matters of law or geography, no humor, no commentary—unless the characters supply them out loud. This is the style in which Dashiell Hammett wrote *The Glass Key* and *The Maltese Falcon*. In both, there are no scenes without the hero. Interestingly, the narrator's position in *The Maltese Falcon* is almost exactly analogous to the camera position in John Huston's film version, eye level, midlength lens, no trick angles.

It's entirely possible to write with the narrator as a camera without sticking to the hero and move from person to person at will. Film scripts are almost universally written that way. George Higgins writes some of his novels that way.

I write primarily in the first person because, for me, it is my natural storytelling voice. It's easy and comfortable.

A story told in the first person means that the reader can see only what the narrator sees. It has a certain inherent excitement, like walking through the night with a flashlight; everything dark except what the beam illuminates. It is akin to how we actually experience life, limited to and locked in one body.

It is helpful in that it limits the selection of what can possibly happen. As a truly omniscient narrator I sometimes feel I have too many choices, too many ways to tell the story, too much possible information that I am responsible for. But locked inside one character I can go only as far and as fast as he or she can go.

I also don't have to know everything. This doesn't matter terribly much if I'm writing about New York, where I do know everything, or close enough. But I had the courage to set *Foreign Exchange* in Austria and Czechoslovakia only because I could hide behind the narrator, who was, like myself, an American. My ignorance and mistakes would be masked. They would even, in a sense, be correct. I'm not talking so much about errors in geography or menu selections but more subtle things, the signs of class and status, the ways culture forms characters, and how subcultures separate people from each other.

I am now writing a book set in England. It's written in the third person. It's much more difficult. Every time I look at the computer screen I am made uneasy by my own ignorance of daily life in this place and of what growing up here really does to a person.

At the same time, the limitations of the first person can be annoying. You can't use information that the narrator wouldn't know. The narrator can't be at every event, so he must learn a lot of stuff secondhand. Some very dramatic events are diluted this way. This is why first-person narratives will often end up with a dramatic third-person prologue, so we can see at first hand the crime that sets the story off.

You lose the ability to show the reader what other characters think and feel. All you have is what the narrator sees them do and hears them say. These characters can tell the narrator what they think and feel—but they frequently lie and distort and don't know. The narrator can imagine what they think and feel, but unlike the writer as omniscient storyteller, the narrator who is a character in the story has self-interest, has limited vision and faults of character. He will lie to himself and may lie to the reader.

If you think for a moment of real life, you realize there are many things that a first-person narrator would never know, would never find out. This leads to all those less-than-credible end scenes in which the antagonist speaks at great, great length about the crime, how it was committed, why it was committed, explaining even those annoying details about what happened to the umbrella with the built-in stiletto, how the glass slipper was broken, and why the formula for making Teflon at home in your very own kitchen didn't actually work.

This does not have to happen. You should know the limits of your story delivery system and build for those limits. Build either a story that can be satisfactorily concluded in terms of only what the narrator sees, or one that is satisfactory even if there are things finally unknown and unresolved.

One of the standard plot mechanisms for building story tension is the contest, the chess game: move vs. countermove. You can't do this in a first-person narration except in the most limited way. In the first-person narration the opponent is more like a baddie in a video game who is visible only when he pops up on-screen and invisible when he pops off again.

Each time I've written in the first person it's been a different experience. The first time it was totally comfortable, like telling my three best personal anecdotes and my two favorite jokes to someone I'd just met who had never heard any of them before. That's always a treat.

The second time I, or the story, absolutely yearned to break loose from the constraints of being locked behind the hero's eyes. I used all kinds of things—songs, newspaper stories both real and bogus, a diary kept by another character—to expand the point of view.

The third time was comfortable but peculiar. The hero didn't really want to "solve" the case. He just wanted to survive and go about his business. Any solution, however incomplete, that permitted him to do that was good enough for him. In the end there were parts of the story that were never told, things that were never explained, because the narrator didn't care. I knew them, but he didn't, so there was no way for me to tell the reader. There was something fun about it.

American Hero, my fourth book, is told partially by a first-person narrator. That character's way of thinking was further from my own. Sustaining that voice, seeing things in ways that I don't see them, feeling things that I don't feel, required a lot of effort and energy. This is part of the fun of being a writer.

Most narratives are normally told in the past tense: *I went, I said, I saw.* Sometimes the story really is in the past and the narrator is looking back. This allows foreshadowing: "When Rex the Wonder Dog walked into my office that day, little did I know that it would change my life forever, end the sale of dog biscuits in Southern Cal, and leave Dora with bite marks on her thigh." The danger with this is that the reader may feel like saying, "If you know all that already, I'd rather you told me now, as succinctly as possible, and get it over with. Terse it, Jack."

But most of the time the past tense is a verbal tic, used because that is the way we speak. The events are dealt with as if they are happening as they are being told, as if what happens next and how the story ends is just being written, one page, at most, ahead of the page we are on.

Sometimes a first-person narrator will use the present tense. There's a logic to it; either we're in the past looking back or we're in the present and we don't know what the next minute will bring. Scott Turow's *Presumed Innocent* is told that way. Jay McInerney used the first-person present in *Bright Lights, Big City* at about the same time, so for a while it seemed like the trendy thing to do. The first-person portion of *American Hero* is present tense, but not as a pretense of immediacy. It was an indication of class and character. Joe, the hero, is that kind of guy, that's the way he talks. Even if he's talking about something that happens twenty years ago, when he's in the jungle, Vietnam, he speaks in the present tense.

Normally it is an awkward voice for both writer and reader.

The third-person present tense—*He kicks the door in. He goes for his gun. Schwantz cowers in the corner. "Shoot me, I deserve to die," Schwantz says, and vomits*—is even more rare. You would think it wouldn't be, since all movies are written in the present tense. Plays, too.

There is no rule for choice of voice. It's a marriage between your personal style and the needs of the story. Once it's chosen, however, you're supposed to remain true. Before you get stressed by the constraints of literary monogamy, let me point out that your choice can be to mix first person and third person. You can do this as is commonly done with third-person prologue followed by a first-person book, or throughout, as Peter Blauner did in *Slow Motion Riot*, or even mix two first persons and one third person as I did in *American Hero*.

Literary rules are soft rules. Like a modern relationship, it has more to do with what you promised up front than what canon law laid down in a previous century.

You can't break out into a third-person aria in the middle of a first-person book. Unless you use a device. *Alibi for an Actress*, by Gillian Farrell, is a standard first-person narration. The investigator/narrator has been assigned to interview everyone who knew the suspect. She tell us:

> *The information came at us in a very random way. If someone wanted to, he could have taken our tapes and by cutting and pasting them together he would have been able to do an audio-only docudrama, The Lucinda Merrill Story. If someone did, it would have looked like this.*

Then she proceeds to give us a biography of the antagonist constructed out of a multivoice narration.

Andrew Klavan, in *True Crime*, which is a work entirely of fiction, has a first-person narrator, a newspaperman who works in the Wolfe/Daley/Breslin New Journalism mode. He interviews people, and once they have told him how they felt at the moment, he writes it the way a novelist would:

> *For several moments after he awoke, he lay as he was, on his side, his eyes closed, facing the wall. His mind gripped at the dream, held onto it with terrible longing. But the dream dissolved mercilessly and, bit by bit, the Deathwatch cell came back to him.*

In short, the person inside the book is a writer, which allows the writer outside the book, Klavan, to have it both ways—first person and third.

Sometimes you get a perfect marriage. *The Maltese Falcon* is one. There is something about the totally objective narrative voice that makes the prose seem set in stone. The story is capable of working itself out in scenes that take place in the present. There is no background given, but there is none needed. There is no exposition except what the characters give to each other. It is never exposition slyly disguised as dialogue inserted to inform the reader. Even Gutman's long speech about the history of the falcon is not there to inform us—the details don't really matter and may not be true—but as his way of manipulating Sam Spade. All the characters lie, freely. And there's no narrator you can trust to sort it out for you.

Lawrence Sanders once wrote a novel, *The Anderson Tapes*, in which everything was heard and/or seen through surveillance equipment. This could have come off as just a gimmick. But, as in a good marriage, he makes both sides work. He comes up with ingenious kinds of surveillance and valid reasons for them to be there. At the same time every incident that he creates to tell the story must occur in a manner and in a place in which it can be electronically observed.

George Higgins maintains a rigorously objective position in his third-person narratives (*The Friends of Eddie Coyle, Cogan's Trade*). He doesn't allow himself even trivial forms of cheating: eyes that "glitter with anger," lips that "twist into a sneer that revealed contempt," nods "of sadness," tears "of despair," smiles "of conciliation." Characters do and characters talk. The result is books that are told through dialogue—he writes *the best* dialogue in the business—with brief spurts of action. The results of this technique can be brilliant. Sometimes it seems mannered, as if the story is stuck behind the demands of having everything revealed through conversation.

Jimmy Breslin writes third-person-omniscient narrations that differ more completely from the third person as used by Hammett or Higgins than they do from a first-person narration. They are rich in internal dialogue, background, sociology, and economics.

In reality when different people talk about the same subject, everything changes. It would make sense that we could have a story told in parts, switching between various narrators, each one with a different world view, different set of references, different way of explaining things, different vocabulary and speaking style. The most successful attempts at this that I have seen are in two nonfiction books created by cutting and pasting interviews with real people: *Edie*, by Jean Stein, edited by George Plimpton, the story of the actress–celebrity–Warhol person Edie Sedgewick, and *Savage Grace*, by Natalie Robins and Steven M. L. Aronson—the "plastics heir kills mother" story.

In fiction I think it would be very difficult to sustain voices that are that different. It's also a strain on the reader. It would be worth doing for the right story, like the film *Rashomon*, in which the very point of the story is how radically it changes when the narrator changes.

In the end you make a choice based on two things: the voice you are most comfortable with combined with the voice needed to tell the story. Some books must be written in the first person, like Jim Thompson's *The Killer Inside Me* and Scott Turow's *Presumed Innocent*. John Mortimer's Rumpole, Raymond Chandler's Philip Marlowe, and many other investigator and lawyer heroes would lose much of their charm in the third person. Sherlock Holmes is told in the second person, by Dr. Watson, so that Watson can marvel at Holmes's brilliance. If it were first person, it would be too egotistical; in true third person it would be annoying. Joseph Wambaugh's *Glitter Dome* and *The New Centurions* are third-person narratives because we need to get inside a multitude of personalities. Jimmy Breslin and Tom Wolfe come to their novels from New Journalism, and it would be a waste to restrict themselves to one character when they've spent their lives figuring out what makes widely different characters tick. Elmore Leonard, with his point, counterpoint plots, needs to be God, and he's an excellent one, terse and economical.

CHAPTER 20

From Cozies to Crime Novels

The index of categories in *Mystery Writer's Marketplace* lists: "Amateur Sleuth, Cozy, Dark Mystery, Espionage, Hard-Boiled Detective, Historical, Humorous Mystery, Juvenile, Light Horror, Malice Domestic, Police Procedural, Private Eye, Romantic Suspense, Surrealistic Mystery, Suspense, Thrillers, Trial Novel, Urban Horror, Young Adult."

Personally, I have a tendency to believe it's all the same stuff. But I'm wrong. Subgenres are important to readers. They are important to publishers. Therefore, at some level, writers should at least be aware of them.

The main two are the cozy and the hard-boiled. The conventions that divide them can be summed up pretty quickly: The hard-boiled has a professional detective, violence and sex, and takes place on the mean streets. The cozy has an amateur sleuth, takes place among "regular" folks, progresses through ratiocination rather than physical action, and sex is not something people do, it's what they have secrets about. But men are growing softer and women are getting tougher and there's lots of crossover and the dividing lines get blurrier. A Muse maturing into androgyny perhaps.

There's a fundamental difference in attitude, however, and this was revealed to me when I first asked people to read this manuscript. Several of them said that I should put in something about cozies.

I'm a reader and a writer, not a scholar or critic. So, for the most part, I read what I like and don't read what I don't like. In fact, I almost can't read what I don't like. I have a prejudice in favor of realism and research. I like sex. I dislike sentiment. I wouldn't exactly say that I like violence, but I got Alexander the Great's point when he cut the Gordian knot. I respond more to politics and money than to family and neighborhood associations. In short, I prefer hard-boiled detective novels to cozies. So much so that I had to ask for help. I asked other writers—through the editors at Ballantine—"What is the appeal of cozies?"

What is the appeal of cozy? Are you nuts? I am a very cynical New Yorker and I enjoy hard-boiled mysteries but I also adore cozies if they are well done. I like them because the characterizations are strong and usually cover a broad range of personalities. The Walter Mitty aspect is also important: most cozy readers are women and so are the heroines. They like to imagine themselves being as resourceful and capable as the detective in the book. Too, cozies take ordinary life situations and strip away the surface to reveal the excitement and seediness beneath. What could be more real in terms of depicting true life? Also, most hard-boiled books are written badly: they try to create a tough tone and atmosphere and fail miserably by appearing posturing. It's hard to fail in terms of a tea cozy because they cover a wider range of acceptable characters and plots and the author is not bound to (ostensible) realism as is the case in hard-boiled and other more realistic genres. Cozies often take a drubbing from critics when it comes to being realistic, and why critics waste time in their reviews taking apart the plots totally perplexes me: cozies require a willing suspension of disbelief. Real crimes are rarely solved through ingenuity and progression. They are solved inadvertently, through revenge or the greed of others involved, or through fate and sometimes the dogged persistence of a detective or team of professionals who refuse to give up long after a book would have drawn to a timely conclusion.

That's from Gallagher Gray. What's interesting is that Gallagher's attitudes and ideas about other aspects of the business are in line with being a cozy fan and a cozy writer. She feels that people read crime fiction

. . . because they are searching for order and flirting with their fears in a very safe manner. They are reassured from the start knowing that the criminal will be caught. . . . This, of course, differs dramatically from the chaotic and unfair order of real life.

Gallagher also feels that the average mystery reader does not want sex.

Sex gets in the way of good plot progression—after all, what could be less logical than sex? And all good mysteries present the logic (in hindsight) that real life lacks. Romance is another story. Softening a hero or killer around the edges and making them more human through romance

is very satisfying. If you do write about sex, subtlety is best. In other words, do it without using a single word associated with sex. That lets readers project their own fantasies into the scene and they get a lot more thrill out of it that way.

I'm aware that there are people who are offended by four-letter words. My books are full of them. Mostly because they have been about people who use them constantly. In fact, my usual procedure when writing dialogue for such characters is to use obscenities about half the time they do and then go back and cut out 90 percent. My mother-in-law still can't read my books and I don't expect her to.

I find the best hard-boiled books don't use the f-words at all, but rather rely on wry humor or cynically erudite articulation of feeling or observations to imprint a unique sense of the character. But there's an even more important reason why I avoid foul language in my harder-core books: I only have x amount of space to tell about the character, whether through their words or their actions. Curse words, while often satisfying in real life, are too commonplace and not distinctive enough to tell you much about the character. I'd rather reserve that space for something a little more unique that gives a hint to the character's inner make-up.

Gallagher Gray

Ellen Hart, who likes cozies and writes cozies, has a similar opinion to Gallagher's about what readers want.

They help make order out of chaos. In real life, good doesn't always triumph over evil. I think people hunger for some kind of order, the kind you rarely find in your everyday existence. . . . Mysteries are our modern morality plays. Good and evil fight it out and good usually wins. The villain is found out, and punished. Order is reestablished.

Jeff Abbott says:

Readers cherish the idea of the good guys winning—a situation that seems to occur less and less frequently in real life.

I find this particularly fascinating because it is not how I had answered the question. I think that they are more in the mainstream than I am. My idea, before I got their letters, was that readers were seeking the satisfaction of vicarious revenge rather than of vicarious order. I had even claimed that the pleasure of seeing order reestablished was a subset of revenge.

My answer went like this: We eat shit every day. We don't like it. There are a great many reasons for accepting it, but no matter how valid they are, none of them are good enough to turn it into Boston cream pie. Mike Hammer never eats it. Sam Spade, Lew Archer, Kinsey Milhone, all those dicks named Cat (or Kat), Parker (the character, not the writer), Travis McGee: you can beat 'em, burn 'em, rape their women (or men), steal their chickens, kill their partners, rip off their buddies, but they always get up, get back in it, and nail the bastards.

The basic structure of an Elmore Leonard plot is that a big tough guy pushes a little tough guy. The little guy doesn't take it. He shoves back. The little guy is the kinda guy, the harder you shove him, the more trouble he's gonna be. In the end, the big guy really wishes he'd picked someone else to shove. When Leonard started he wrote westerns, and in those early books you can see the bones without an X ray. I recommend *Valdez Is Coming* to anyone who wants to understand the structure of an Elmore Leonard novel.

The same skeleton is beneath the skin of a Dick Francis novel. The shoving sequence is at least part of the plot of most hard-boiled detective novels. It might start with a case, but it becomes a *little-guy-not-takin'-crap-from-no-one* story when someone tries to strong-arm the shamus to stop him from snooping.

Throughout *The Godfather*, characters keep saying, "It's not personal, it's business." Which is a way of saying, control yourself, there are sufficient countervailing interests—money, survival, money, survival—for you to eat the injury or insult. Until Michael Corleone decides to kill the man who tried to kill his father.

> " . . . *don't let anybody kid you. It's all personal, every bit of business. Every piece of shit every man has to eat every day of his life is personal. They call it business. OK. But it's personal as hell.*"

Oh, how gratifying that is. That's why the gangster is better than the businessman—or at least we feel that way somewhere in our hearts—because mere money, mere survival, isn't enough to make him eat shit.

Perhaps that is the fundamental difference between the cozy and the hard-boiled.

Another difference is supposed to be that cozies are English and hard-boileds are American. Oddly, this is a truth. If you go into an English bookstore, the books in the mystery section are cozier than they are in America. English writers write cozy books. Sometimes they try to write hard-boiled.

They don't succeed. It's a cozy country. America ain't. You can take that to the bank, motherfucker.

The heyday of the cozy was the "Golden Age," when a mystery was not a soul-searing journey down mean and sleazy streets, awash in despair and degradation, it was to be a "fair-play puzzle," and the pleasure taken from it was something rather like doing the *Times* crossword puzzle. The quintessential situation was a locked-room murder. The writer's job was to plant clues. The reader's job was to figure out the puzzle before the end. A good one was a "near thing" in the race between the reader and the sleuth, but the writer had to "play fair," and the clues by which the sleuth came to his conclusion had to be equally available to the reader, and it had to be possible to come to that solution from those clues.

Cozies are still, in some degree, supposed to be fair-play mysteries, a game of clues and conclusions in which the solution, no matter how improbable and rickety, is fine so long as it can be constructed out of the bits and pieces of informational Tinkertoy scattered with assiduous cunning in the grasses of the country lawn around the country home where the murder most foul took place.

Structurally, however, the cozy and the hard-boiled are still members of the same family—the story is an investigation and the question is whodunit. Thrillers and legal thrillers have their own framework based around the contest, but even so, more often than not, the trial is an excuse for an investigation and as a climax, the revelation of who really dunit. Just the way it always happened with Perry Mason.

The crime novel and the cop novel frequently, though not always, depart from the whodunit-investigation structure. Take a look at Joseph Wambaugh (*The New Centurions, The Choirboys, The Blue Knight*), Robert Leuci (*Fence Jumpers, Captain*

Butterfly), Tom Wolfe (*Bonfire of the Vanities*), Jimmy Breslin (*The Gang That Couldn't Shoot Straight*), Michael Dibdin (*Tryst, Dirty Tricks*), George Higgins (*The Digger's Game, Cogan's Trade, The Rat on Fire, Kennedy for the Defense*), Patricia Highsmith (*The Talented Mr. Ripley, Strangers on a Train*), Jim Thompson (*The Killer Inside Me, The Grifters*), Peter Blauner (*Slow Motion Riot*), and Richard Price (*Clockers*). Dibdin, Leuci, Wambaugh, and Higgins have, by the way, done books that are structured around an investigation, so the difference is not compulsive or genetic. It is one of choice.

The investigation can be a crutch. Drop the crutch and you have to walk on the two legs of character and situations. In the investigation novel, the detective stands between us and the crime; the process of uncovering character and action supersedes the actuality of character and action. In the legal thriller we also take one step away from life. Blood and chaos are reorganized, after the fact, into a game. The expression of emotions and the choice of actions are held in check by ritual formalities. Take the lawyer and the investigator away and the writer has to get in there and deal with the passions and the acts face-to-face.

CHAPTER 21

Editors & Editing

When Harvey Ginsberg at William Morrow told my agent that he would buy my first book, he also told her that I would have to cut it in half. Although I didn't think the book could stand a full 50 percent reduction in size, I also had to consider that I had $36.50 in the bank and the rent was a week overdue. I said I would like to talk to Mr. Ginsberg directly and find out what he wanted cut and why. If there was reason in his request, I would, I said, look at the manuscript with sincerity and see if it could survive major surgery.

We spoke. He wanted the book cut to no more than ninety thousand words because, as it was a first mystery, he felt certain he could sell about 3,200 copies at $16.95. If the book were larger, it would cost more to produce and ship and he would therefore have to sell 4,000 copies or charge $17.95, neither of which he felt certain he could do. So there was reason and good sense in his request. It was valid and I respected it.

As a neophyte author and unfamiliar with the folkways, I had typed my manuscript this way, single-spacing lines, double-spacing paragraphs.

When Mr. Ginsberg calculated my word count he had not taken that into account. A word about word count. It's not. It's what the word count would be if each page held only the middle of a single paragraph; that is to say, as if it were wall-to-wall words of average size.

I came to the realization that my manuscript was about 135,000 words, not the 180,000 to 200,000 that Harvey had estimated. I therefore only had to cut my book by a third. Compared to cutting it in half, that seemed well within the realm of possibility.

I called Mr. Ginsberg back. I didn't know it at the time but he is frequently referred to as "the legendary Harvey Ginsberg." He is much revered and even in retirement he edits John Irving and gets thanked for it on the thank-you page, and I acquired some cachet by being published by him. I announced the news of the wondrous miscount and said that I could in all probability make the cuts. "What," I inquired, "do you suggest I cut?" I had been raised on the Maxwell Perkins legend—which we all sort of know even if we don't know it by name—of fevered creative collaboration, the editor portrayed as a calm and incisive Olympian who could guide the demonic but untutored verbal energies of rabid and foaming young authors—like F. Scott Fitzgerald, Ernest Hemingway, and Thomas Wolfe—into tempered acts of genius, reshaping the raw power of base metal into the finest hammered steel in the manner of Japanese sword makers.

"You're the writer," Harvey said. "You decide."

My first reaction—on the basis of my romantic illusions and a certain laziness—was disappointment. I was a blind man assigned to lead myself.

In retrospect it was very good advice indeed. In the first place, the book was vastly improved by losing thirty thousand words. I constantly read books that make me wish they had been edited with the same casually dictatorial ruthlessness. In the second place, when Harvey finally did make suggestions, I hated them.

It is important to understand what an editor is. The position of editor is not—for the most part, and in my experience—an artistic function. It is a business function. An editor works for a publishing company. It is his job to acquire publishable manuscripts, estimate correctly how many copies can be sold with what amount of money and effort, then to pitch the book internally. That is, make a case in competition with all the other editors and their books, getting as big a slice of the company's dollar-and-effort pie as he can for his books. The editor also has to pitch the salespeople (that's what happens at sales conferences), the PR people, and so on. From the writer's point of view, the editor is the book's representative and manager inside the publishing company.

There is a management portion of the job as well. This consists of coordinating all the details and schedules and personnel or at least staying in some sort of communication with the various parties. In the ordinary run of things this is reasonably routine and the writer doesn't have to worry about it. Of course, as soon as anything nonroutine shows up, like a graphic, the system stutters and stumbles and spews up a continual stream of flaws.

The wonderful thing about publishing is that it's cheap to publish a book. Especially compared to producing a motion picture or television program or recording an album. There may be fewer and fewer publishing companies, but each editor is still an independent little fiefdom, so there are lots of people to submit to and lots of opinions, and the result is, a lot of different books get published.

Once the decision to publish any given book is made, the attitude becomes primarily concerned with the downside risk. The rule of thumb is to expend enough money and energy to get back the investment in the book. The goal of a publishing company that has acquired a first novel for $6,000 to $8,000 dollars is to sell 3,200 hundred hardcover copies and make a paperback sale of $15,000 dollars. They keep half the paperback money. You can figure that out.

They will spend what it takes—very little—to accomplish that. And then they will stop. Any sales over that figure are sort of up to the book to accomplish by itself. The goal of a publishing company that has acquired a book for $600,000 dollars is to sell a proportionately higher number of copies, but not quite so many as they need to sell for a million-dollar book. Publishers are not—as a rule—looking for "a find," a ten-thousand-dollar book that they can sell as if it were a million-dollar book. It confuses them. When a book that's not expected to take off does , as often as not, the publisher fumbles it. They can't print more books or they can't ship them or they've misplaced their warehouse.

There are several reasons for this. All of them valid. First is the belief that if the book could sell like a million-dollar book, lots of people would have agreed on that and bid it up that high at auction. If your editor is the only one in the world who thinks your first novel could be a bestseller and nobody else agreed with him enough to bid against him, he would be pretty dumb to risk his future at the company by convincing them to kick Robert Ludlum or Jackie Collins or

John Le Carré from number one on the fall list and put you there. Second is that publishing house resources are not all that flexible in comparison to their production and their lists. Their million-dollar advertising, sales, and promotion budget has to be committed to insuring (as much as it can be insured) that their million-dollar acquisition earns out. If a book makes back costs, its acquiring editor is safe. Anything that earns back over cost, by itself, without requiring any additional investment (more risk) to get there is pure profit.

This is why one of the worst things that can happen to an author is to get orphaned, an expression that means that your acquiring editor is no longer with the firm.

Steve Womack sold his first novel to an editor who got into a fight with her boss and got fired. The boss then told Steve his book was "tiresome," and canceled his contract. When an editor says something like that, it's really hard not to believe it. Until the same book, published by a different house, makes the *New York Times* Notable Book list, as Womack's *Murphy's Fault* did.

More often you will be kept. When an editor inherits your orphan, it will be his lowest priority. Or lower. This is virtually impossible to overcome. In part because most editors will lie to your face about it. Your editor is scrambling desperately to get money and position for the books he acquired. If your book fails, all blame falls on the person dumb enough to have bought it, not on the poor editor who has inherited the idiot's mistakes.

In publishing it's always the book that fails, just as to authors it is always the marketing, advertising, and distribution that failed the book.

This is also why, in the general way of things, when your book gets all those great reviews, the publisher does nothing. I have heard editors, and agents parroting the editors, say,

"Reviews don't sell books." As the author instinctively suspects, this is a way of saying, "Don't bother me, kid. Go away." Actually, a book's share of advertising and marketing, and its position on the publisher's list, have been set in stone long before even the reviews in *Kirkus* and *Publishers Weekly* come out. Sometimes, if a publisher has been considering giving a slight push to a book in which they have only a small investment, negative reviews will discourage them. Sometimes, if a book makes a ton of money, a publisher will plow a portion of it back into advertising and promotion, the book having already paid for the added expense. It is more likely, however, that any greater investment will be put toward your next book in much the way a successful athlete doesn't earn any more for a great season but gets it for the next season. Or rather, the first upcoming season in which he is not already under contract.

This is not solely a publishing phenomenon. The more something sells, the more it's advertised. While some advertising in the wider world of consumer goods goes to new product introductions, the bulk of it goes to established products—Coke, Pepsi, Ford, GM, Budweiser, Tide, Ludlum, Turow, Le Carré, Collins.

What do editors want? Which is another way of saying, what do editors think sells books?

Bestselling authors sell books. Now more than ever. If the hardcover and paperback bestseller lists are combined, John Grisham, Michael Crichton, and Anne Rice are each capable of having four or five of their books on the list at once. There's a group of writers whose every book automatically makes the list. And a lot of them are crime writers. To a certain degree, once you're on the list, you stay there.

What else? Celebrity authors (lot of good that does you). Celebrity subjects. Series. Editors really like series characters because they hope a series can build a following, all by itself, with not too much of an investment on the part of the publishing house. Clones. A current big clone category is legal thrillers. I would guess that all things being equal, most mass-market publishing companies with a legal thriller will put a scales of justice on the cover, give it a title as close to *The Firm* as they can, and push it a lot harder than a straight novel or some other form of crime novel, irrespective of quality. The big clone categories change. In the last few years we've had women detectives and techno-thrillers. There will be more.

Finally there is the "hot book." *Presumed Innocent* was one. These get picked before reviews, before publication, even before their sale to a publisher. They are selected as rumors. I'm not quite sure how. For years I begged my agent to start a rumor that my new book was "the hot book." Either she didn't or no one listened.

A big movie sale, which usually happens long before publication, can make a book a hot book. This happened to *A Simple Plan* and to *The Firm*.

There are editors, and they are very few, who can break an author out. They are usually the head of the company with a lot of discretion and not too many people to answer to. I suspect it is this elite group that controls the "hot book" rumors. But even they can't guarantee it. Sonny Mehta at Knopf (disguised as Pantheon), along with Oliver Johnson at Random House–U.K. and Helge Malchow at Kiepenheuer & Witsch (Germany), were good enough to me to take a shot at it with *American Hero*. Not an all-out, million-dollar shot, but a pretty good one, and it never made the bestseller lists.

I have spent my entire career trying to influence editors to expend more effort, energy, and money, in more intelligent ways, on promoting my books. I have been ingratiating, sometimes sarcastic, helpful, patient, pleading, hypocritical, and have had as much impact as a single drop of water on a rock. I have yet to move one of them an inch. Even when they love my work and are putting money and effort into it, it has nothing to do with me as a person and as a sycophant.

Once you get to paperback and the publisher has decided where on his or her list to stick you, there is only one thing your publisher can do for you—or against you—and that's your cover. I repeat the story that was told to me by Bob Leuci, ex-cop, excellent writer, and a producer at *A Current Affair*. Bob's publisher was going to send him on a book tour. Bob, trying to be clever, trying, like me, to find the point, any point, where he could influence this process to bring him out of writer obscurity into writer celebrity, or at least decent sales figures, said, "Don't send me to the bookstores, send me to the distributors, the jobbers, the guys who decide what books go on the racks at the supermarket and the drugstores." So they sent him. Bob began to tell the jobbers and distributors why his book was special: its technique, its content, its appeal to readers. "Nah, nah," they said. "You don't understand. Some of the books, your real bestsellers, they automatically go up front. John Grisham, Elmore Leonard, what have you. Then say we got ten spots left. We get two hundred new books a month. We rip a cover offa one of each of 'em. We take all the covers and tack 'em up on the wall there. Then we go across the room and we look. We go, 'That one . . . that one . . . and that one.' That's how we pick the books that go on the rack."

CHAPTER 22

Promotion & Self-Promotion, Career, Luck & Sincerity, Agents, Miscellaneous Rules

Your publisher will promote you to the degree that they have committed to promoting you. Which could well be not at all. I went to a panel at a Bouchercon, which is the biggest of the many mystery conventions. The speakers were primarily publishers' PR people, and the subject was "What to expect from your publisher's PR department," or something quite similar. They spoke of varying degrees of help. Simple things like setting up signings, sending releases to your hometown papers, and more, which I forget at the moment.

I felt like I had stumbled into a parallel universe. (This was before *American Hero*.)

I would say, as a rule of thumb, expect nothing from them. Do not expect them to listen to your brilliant marketing suggestions. Even if they are making a major push for you— book tour, interviews, special reader's editions—they will do it their way. Do not expect them to submit your books to contest judges, even if you're a previous winner. If they do any of those things, that's real lagniappe. *Lagniappe* is a New Orleans word; it means a little something extra, something for nothing, like the thirteenth doughnut in a baker's dozen, but sexier.

If you are the sort of person equipped to self-promote, do it. I am told that making the rounds really helps. Going from bookstore to bookstore, from mystery convention to mystery convention, being nice, being friendly, promoting your own work locally, developing mailing lists, sending out postcards. There is a level where hand-selling books is really important—the mystery bookstores and the independents—and that is where the core of your readership shops and where you can build a following.

The main mystery conventions are Bouchercon, Left Coast Crime, which both move around, Malice Domestic in the Washington-Baltimore area (P.O. Box 71, Herndon, VA 22070), The Mystery Writers of America Annual Conference and Edgar Awards Banquet (MWA, 17 E. 47th Street, New York, NY 10017), and the Southwest Mystery Convention. There seem to be more every year. The schedules, locations, and addresses appear in various mystery magazines and newsletters.

Sisters in Crime has an excellent brochure called "Shameless Promotion for Brazen Hussies." There are electronic bulletin boards on the Internet. CompuServe has a Literary Forum with a Mystery section and a Crime Forum with a Writing section. Lary Crews's piece on writing, which I got from CompuServe, has quite an extensive and very useful account of his own self-promotion efforts.

The biggest and oldest crime writers group is Mystery Writers of America. You can become an affiliate member without having been published. Their counterpart in the U.K. is CWA, Crime Writers' Association, but they take only published writers. They can be reached through their secretary: Anthea Fraser, Owlswick 22 Chiltern Way, Tring, Herts, HP23VJK. My favorite is the International Crime Writers of America (JAF Box 1500, New York, NY 10116) because we meet in places like Gijón, Spain, and Prague, Czech Republic, and also because I like foreigners almost as much as I like being a foreigner. Sisters in Crime's address is P.O. Box 442124, Lawrence, KS 66044-8933. Men are accepted. American Crime Writers League is at 12 St. Ann Drive, Santa Barbara, CA 93109. The Private Eye Writers of America is at 330 Surrey Road, Cherry Hill, NJ 08002. All of them have newsletters and various informational and member services.

If you're really serious about self-promotion, the time to do it is before you even sell your book. Probably before you write it. Invent a name and persona like Madonna or Bob Dylan or Prince. Gillian Farrell, for example, invented a persona, though not with malice aforethought, the actress-detective. Books by real cops and real law enforcement persons and real Mafiosos appeal to publishers and especially to promotion departments because there is a hook, something to promote. Readers like it too. They think they're getting the inside dope. Authentico. I don't know if any of the ex-cops out there are fake, maybe they are, and if not, maybe you should be the first. I wouldn't fake a big-city PD, like New York or Chicago or L.A., but pick somewhere small where they don't read books and don't go to your (fake) home on book tour. Or you could invent a past as a criminal. Though prisoner books do break out from time to time, I think going to prison, especially a maximum-security joint, which is where the good drama happens, for a long stay, in order to get a book out of it, is probably an exercise in excess. But you might be able to get away with claiming that you are an escapee and can't give your real name because you're still wanted. They can't use your picture because you've had plastic surgery. Or you could say that you were in the Mexican mob in Guadalajara. Or you were in SAVAK, the Shah's secret police. Four or five words of Farsi should handle anyone who challenges your identity. Another way to go it is to get a friend who is a cop or DEA agent or some such and borrow his identity.

The sensible Cathy Repetti, my editor, suggests that these scenarios are too off-the-wall. That I should suggest developing a unique though manageable personal history.

Between that suggestion and this revision, *Sleepers*, by Lorenzo Caracaterra, was published. It purports to be, and was published as, a true story. With the names changed to protect the guilty. It was sold to Propaganda Films, a division of Polygram, before publication, for two million dollars, and it was announced that several major actors had been signed for it. Publishers around the world paid large sums for it. It is the story of four boys who were sent to reform school, where they were beaten and raped by the guards. One of them grew up to be a reporter and the book's author, one a prosecutor in the New York DA's office, and two of them became mob killers. Ten years later the mobsters found the guard and executed him in front of witnesses. They then conspired with the DA and the author to create a misprision of justice in the name of natural justice.

After publication, naturally, other reporters began to search for the real players and the actual records. Nobody could find anything. Not even anything remotely similar that could have been transplanted or transposed. A chorus of voices arose claiming the book was fiction and condemning Caracaterra.

As far as I know, nobody's asked him to give the money back.

Irrelevant celebrity helps as much or more than relevant celebrity. We have both a Truman and a Roosevelt writing mysteries. They get considerably greater distribution than they would if they were written by Quatrochocci or Lip-schitz. Steve Allen, the comedian, Kinky Friedman, the country music singer, Gary Hart, and one of the Quayles have all parlayed a little name power into the mystery game.

On the other hand, I came into this biz from the commercial film biz. The horror of the film biz is that the ratio of wheedling, begging, schmoozing, and scheming to be permitted to work to actually working is at least 100:1. The glory of writing is that you don't need anyone's goddamn permission to do it. It doesn't cost ten million dollars to borrow a typewriter and to find an office or institution that won't miss a few reams of paper. Then the work pretty much speaks for itself. You can be ugly, obnoxious, foulmouthed, foul breathed. You can be a man who shaves his legs or a woman who shaves her face, you can be anorexic or obese, be flatulent and having eating disorders—and it doesn't matter. Or at least not that much. Don't expect to go on tour.

LUCK

There is luck in this business. Good and bad.

I've been very lucky. With my first book I got an agent, I got published in hardcover, I won an Edgar. I've been unlucky. *Time* magazine was scheduled to do a story on me when *American Hero* was published. They sent a photographer. She took my picture. I looked too fat, but I could've lived with that. Then Toni Morrison won the Nobel Prize. That was their book story for the week. I got bumped into never-was-and-soon-forgotten land. The PR person from Pantheon went to the *New York Times* and discovered that I was going to be reviewed in the genre ghetto, the "Spies and Thrillers" column, and told them, oh no, this is a big book, it should be reviewed like a real novel. The *Times* said yes and took it from one pile, put it on another pile, and it never got reviewed in the *New York Times*.

Another novelist I know had 250,000 copies published of his first novel, a paperback original. I happen to know his publisher, and I asked, "Why?" since there didn't seem to be anything about the book that stood out that much. The editor told me he had happened to have a hole at the top of his list that period, remembered this book, and figured he could put a legal thriller clone cover on it. A lot of books went out, they got prominent positions in the stores, and they did, in fact, sell. So on the author's second book, they put out 300,000. And so on.

Justin Scott knew he had a hit when he finished *Ship Killer*. He made an outright movie sale. The publisher put it at the top of their list. The film company and the publisher and Justin put up fifty thousand dollars each for an ad campaign. Two weeks before the book came out, the *New York Times* went on strike. There was no place to put the money. The book sold well enough to be on the *New York Times* bestseller list—but there wasn't one.

Bookstores frequently have sections for books that have been movies and television shows. Dillons, a British chain, now has a section next to the mystery section that features "TV Detectives." Inspector Morse and Spenser, among others, clearly owe some portion of their books' success to their television careers.

Publishers will tell you that it takes three or four or five books to build yourself a name, to break out. The number varies, but it is always one more than the one you're on. Presumably there is a number that you get to, perhaps seven or eight, when they get to say, "It's hopeless. If you haven't broken out by now, you probably won't, and we can't take the chance."

Editors like series because they can hope, and they can tell you, that a series builds itself. This takes them off the hook.

I won't say that you can't make yourself lucky, but I sure as hell can't tell you how. But there is enough room in this business that if you keep at it, you can earn yourself a niche. If you keep at it longer and pay attention to what you do and to people's reactions to it and to what the books are like that sell better than yours, you can make that niche slowly bigger.

SINCERITY

Two of the biggest bestsellers of the nineties are *Bridges of Madison County* and *The Celestine Prophecies*. Both are regarded by the literary establishment as awful. *The Celestine Prophecies* was regarded as so awful that no one would publish it. It was self-published. (This is not an argument for going the vanity press route. *The Celestine Prophecies* is the only vanity publication that I've ever heard of that ended that way.)

The people who wrote them believe in them. They believe that they are of great literary quality. They believe that what they have to say matters. They believe that other people are failing to say it and it needs saying.

You have to do the best writing you can.

You may have selected genre writing because it does not intimidate you. You don't have to be Hemingway, Shakespeare, Dickens, Joyce. That's a good reason. But given that, you have to write the best book you can write.

AGENTS

It's better to have an agent than not.

You may think that they are taking 10 or 15 percent of your money and you will make more money by not having an agent. This is very unlikely.

Editors read submissions from agents much, much faster than those from writers. Editors answer phone calls from agents.

To say that a publisher's standard boilerplate contract is designed to rob you blind and steal back anything they might have given you by mistake is an exaggeration. But they are certainly not based on fairness, not infused with a spirit of generous giving, and not what a book writers' union would demand if we had one. There are clauses that they will be truly adamant about. There are others that they're just trying on. If you accept them, that's your problem. I don't know which ones are which. My agent does.

Contracts are written, for the most part, in ass-backward legal gobble. If you have to read only one a year or every couple of years, it's not worth the weeks of effort it takes to understand one. Agents have to read them regularly. They ought to be able to look at them the way a chef looks at a recipe.

Editors and publishers like dealing with agents. They understand each other. They don't have to go over the same old basics. They don't have to have fights that there is no point in having.

If a publisher offers to buy your first book from a direct submission, they may also suggest that you get an agent to do the deal. They may recommend one. That's not as negative and collusive a thing as you might think it is. At that point it will be easy to get an agent, the one they recommend or a different one. Even one who does not look at submissions and does not take on new clients.

The way to get an agent is to write a book. Then find a friend who has an agent. Give the book to the friend and ask him if it's "suitable" for his agent. That gives your friend a gracious out so he can say after he's read it: "No, my agent is not taking on any crime writers." This is important if you want to stay on speaking terms with your friend. After you've exhausted personal contacts, *Writer's Market* and *Mystery Writer's Marketplace*, various other writers' publications and some of the mystery writers' organizations have lists of agents who will read submissions.

Writers don't pay agents. Not to read their manuscript. Not for nothin'.

Agents collect a percentage of the gross amounts they collect from sales they make of a writer's work. They may also deduct additional small amounts for specific, documented expenses that do not include the normal cost of doing business or general overhead.

MISCELLANEOUS

1. Double-space your manuscript.
2. Send out clean, legible, typed manuscripts.
3. Have copies of your manuscript. In these days of word processors and copiers and floppy disks and hard drives, this should not even have to be mentioned.
4. Never eat at a restaurant called Mom's, collect all possible receipts, don't buy drugs from people with guns.

CHAPTER 23

Better

If I had to give one rule, separate and apart from all the rest written here, for writing better, it would be: Make every scene worth reading for its own sake.

Furthering the plot is not sufficient reason, alone, for retaining more than a sentence.

The scene should have some value beyond movement. It should have its own merit—make us laugh or weep, stimulate our intellect with fresh perspectives and new ideas, teach something, give us a rooting interest, threaten us, put us on the edge of our seats, make us get up and check to see if the doors are locked and the kids are safely in bed. Whatever. It's got to do something more than move the characters across the chessboard.

This statement assumes that you've already dealt with all the other stuff discussed in the previous pages. Narrative Drive being the most necessary part of what you do, and

Clarity being the most important aspect of how you do it. Scene Construction is a subset of Narrative Drive, and an Opening is a subset of Scene Construction. Using Hooks is a technique.

Plotting is—frequently—strenuous and difficult work, more noticeable when it fails than when it succeeds, and to the degree that it is separate from narrative drive, much the harder of the two. And plotting is very much a dictator. It says there are things you can't do and things you must do.

Plotting fails when you fail to work through to an action or a conclusion that makes real human sense for the characters in the scene. What is called flimsy, cardboard and thin happens when you do something that satisfies a plot point but does it in a way that is not suitable for the people you've created.

Gillian Farrell, my wife, says, "Inspiration." My knee-jerk reaction is to disagree because she is my wife, because this is symptomatic of our different ways of looking at the world, and because this is a "how-to" book and how can I say, "The way to write a better book is to go out and get some inspiration"? However, as in most things she says, there is merit and possibility.

Writing a book is hard work. It is a long, arduous task. Straining to make it a better book, refusing to settle for adequate solutions, takes even more energy. "Inspiration," an emotional involvement in the work, whether that is love or money or competitiveness or recognition hunger or anger or grief, certainly helps to supply the kind of mental energy that writing requires.

Although I truly believe that I can write a book about anything by following my own rules, and perhaps I will someday on a dare, in fact, I pick subjects that somehow "inspire" me. As a practical matter, how does one find material that inspires? You keep looking and making lists. Or you run, literally, until so much oxygen is pumped into your brain that you start to think. Or you run out of money. Or you go to a different place so that your mind opens up to new possibilities. And when you're actually writing a book, you look inside for your anger and love, humiliation and sorrow, satisfactions and hungers. Feel them, cultivate them, wallow in them, bestow them on people in your pages.

REWRITING

First—a warning. Finishing is the most important thing.

Finishing is more important than perfection, polish, and rewriting. More important, especially, than a great first line, paragraph, page, or chapter. Get it done. Fix it later. People have spent their lives perfecting a first page; many a writing life has died there.

A lot of writers do a casual daily rewrite. They start the day by rewriting what they did yesterday. It helps to read it out loud. Among other things this will make you read what you actually wrote rather than what you think you wrote.

When you've finished the book you probably want to take a break. Fine, go have a cup of coffee. Come back in twenty minutes, a week, a month, whatever you need. Then read the book out loud. Every word. Simplify what you can't get your tongue around. Cut when you get bored. Stop when you get tired. There is a difference.

Presumably at this point you will pick up on your mechanical errors: names that change in midbook, timings that are impossible, people who grow shorter and taller. You will find scenes that need more clarity, others that need more subtlety, clues that could be better hidden, characters that need some detail, motivations that need clarification. If you have a cast list and an outline that you revised as you wrote, you'll want it with you when you do this. If you haven't made them, you might want to now.

When you were doing your first draft you may well have put in a scene that was just so-so in order to move the plot or to have conflict because every scene should have conflict. That's OK, because moving forward and finishing was important then. This is now. This is the time to make it better.

In *No One Rides for Free* I had a scene in which the hero goes to speak to the police. A scene with conflict is better than a scene of amity. I had written the scene in which The Cop says, "Listen, shamus, this is police business. We don't take to sleazy keyhole peepers in this town. Keep your nose out of it." Ugh! Stupid. Boring. But I wrote it to get through that part of the necessary procedure. When I reread it, it was still Ugh! Stupid. Boring. It was the worst scene in the book. So I gave the difficult cop, the chief of police, a reason to be difficult. There was a missing child. The chief was running around the county following a psychic from Nutley, New Jersey, who said the body was by a body of water and a lightnin'-struck tree. I had never read that scene before. Some stuff you have to come at sideways.

When it sounds bad, it is bad. Change it.

After you've done that, have as many people read it as you can. Friends and relations. Tell them to be as heartless and cruel as possible. You want to know if and when they were bored. What scenes they liked and what they didn't like. What they didn't understand. What they felt.

Now here's the hard part. Shut up and listen. Take notes. Your defense mechanisms will kick in and want to justify and explain. Shut up. Don't. That's not what you're there for. The notes are for later when the voice inside you—which didn't shut up—finally does shut up and you can then find out what it was your friends told you.

They're right, you're wrong. They're the customers. They're the focus group that represents the audience. They're the people on the other side of the conversation. This is a chance to really hear them, not just imagine them. If they say they didn't understand something, that's true, they didn't understand it. If they told you they didn't like something, it is unequivocally true. They didn't like it.

It is your job to fix what they didn't understand. It's no good saying they're stupid. If you're a good writer, you can make things so clear that even people as stupid as your spouse—who is willfully stupid, doing it just to drive you berserk—can understand it.

If they say they hated the hero, it is indisputably true that they hated him. If you don't want them to hate him, then you have to change him. There's no defense. You can't travel with the book and explain to the readers why they should have loved the hero. You have to find a way to make readers feel the hero is heroic, lovable, admirable, worth rooting for and caring about.

The oddity is that when they tell you why they didn't like or understand something, and how to fix it, they are always wrong. They don't really know why they don't like what they don't like, and they don't know how to fix it.

You have to figure it out.

For example: They might say they didn't like your hero because he kills someone and they can't like a person who kills. Do you take out the killing or do you work at the situation, the buildup, until the reader's reaction is "Yeah, Do it! Slaughter the pig!" They might say they didn't like your hero because he is an adulterer. Again, you might feel that he has to be. You must alter the circumstances so that the readers approve, understand, or forgive.

Your editor and your agent are professional readers. But still just readers. This goes for them, too. They're accurate and right about their reactions, not necessarily the reasons for their reactions.

Nonetheless, you have to listen to the part where they tell you how they think it's wrong and how to fix it. There will be clues in there that help you pinpoint the problem.

There are exceptions. Sometimes one person will react badly to something in your book. If ten or twenty people loved the exact same thing, you might consider keeping it. Sometimes a reader will be right about how to fix something. Sometimes you draw to an inside straight.

Your job is to make the book work on people the way you want it to work. When I teach skiing and I have incompetent, unlearning, fearful students who want to quit without even trying, I beg them to stay and tell them, "Teaching skiing is not like teaching in school. School is all about students who fail. Here, only the teacher can fail." Your readers can't fail you. Only you can fail them.

CHAPTER 24

Doing It

Doing it is what it's all about. It's terribly absolute. You do it or you don't. You get from page one to page last with a story and a bunch of words in between. You start and you keep going until it's over. Or you don't.

> *The writer who gets published is the writer who finishes the book.*
>
> Ellen Hart

WORKING

I aim for a number of pages per day. And I try to put in a full workday, just like a real person who goes to an office and does real work. At the same time, if I don't know what is going to happen next, I don't write. I try very hard to figure it out, but I don't write. Sometimes writing down possibilities helps. Sometimes I look to the original proposal, sometimes to my bag of stuff that I wanted to include. Sometimes I run; while I run I zone out and ideas come up.

For me, the deciding what to write is the big thing and the difficult thing. Writing it is comparatively easy. This may not be true for everyone. Many people may experience the opposite, easy to decide, hard to execute. Or some variation thereof.

If I were a great, quick, and easy plotter, but had trouble with dialogue and style and description, I suspect that the way I would approach things is to write a fast first draft and then build through rewrites.

I am in the habit of starting the day by rereading and rewriting whatever I wrote the day before. It gets me back in the groove and gives me a feeling of having accomplished something.

Everybody has their own method and habits and tricks.

1—Write every day. Don't wait for inspiration. Write even when you're tired and you would much rather do anything else.

2—Don't start rewriting on a book until you have completed a first draft. If you can't complete a first draft, you will NEVER complete a book. Too much rewriting early on is a delaying tactic.

3—Set a target date on your calendar to have the manuscript completed. Honor this date as if it were a formal business obligation.

Jeff Abbott

A regular schedule, setting a daily goal, reaching it, seem to be the essentials common to almost all of us.

WRITER'S BLOCK

This is one of the great mythologies. By that I don't mean that it's not true or that it doesn't happen. But it's something like frigidity in women. (Oh boy, this metaphor is trouble on the wing.) Anyway, there are no more frigid women, just preorgasmic women. It used to be that women were expected to climax through genital intercourse. Then women started examining themselves with a new frankness and honesty and Masters and Johnson attached wires and electrodes to various organs and it was discovered that the problems were not Freudian, they were mechanical. It wasn't that a woman was dysfunctional, it was how she was being handled. Handled right, we can all make it. So with writer's block. I hope. And pray.

Larry Block, in *Writing the Novel*, tells this story. It is dear to my heart because it fits my experience.

> A friend of mine was on a television talk show with several other mystery writers, Mickey Spillane among them. After the program ended, Spillane announced that they'd neglected to talk about the most important topic. "We didn't say anything about money."
>
> ... He'd spent several years on an offshore island ... where he did nothing too much more taxing than swim and sunbathe and walk the beach. ... "Every once in a while it would come to me that it'd be fun to get started on a book," he said. "I thought I'd keep my mind in shape and I'd enjoy doing it. But I could never get a single idea for a story. I'd sit and sit, I'd walk for miles, but I couldn't get an idea.
>
> "Then one day I got a call from my accountant to say that the money was starting to get low. Nothing serious,

*but I should start thinking about ways to bring in some
dough. And boy did I get ideas for books!"*

My block comes in deciding what book to write. I can
dither over that for years. So far the only way I've found to
overcome this loitering about, dysfunctionally, is to run out
of money. I can write like hell when I'm broke. I'm trying to
learn to get ahead of myself. I've got two young children to
support.

The one kind of preorgasmic condition I can't tell you how
to get past is my own. For the others I have excellent advice.

If, when you start, you know the beginning and the end,
you can't get too stuck. Or I should say, when I've known the
beginning and the end, I've never gotten stuck for too long.
That's the kind of thing, you say it the wrong way, it turns
around and bites you next time out of the stable.

First, psych yourself up to it. From Larry Block—"On your
worst day, you can write one page." You might have to
throw it out. You might have to change it. But you can write
one page.

Don't know what to write? Here are some things you can
write:

1. A list of the characters and what they want at that point
   in the story. Once you know what they want, imagine that
   you are each of them in turn, and figure out what they're
   going to do about it.
2. Look at your list of high points and scenes you want to
   see. Write one of them, even if it's out of sequence.
3. Write what has to lead up to one of those scenes. Not
   necessarily in the form of the book. It can be in the form
   of notes and suggestions.
4. Do a biography of one of the characters that you haven't
   done yet.

5. Do some form of mindless repetitive intense exercise that doesn't require your complete and intricate attention. Do it for a long time.

6. Go and do some more research. If it's appropriate. Write out what you've discovered in essay or action form.

7. Try to figure out what the problem is. Sometimes you stop because there is an actual problem in the story. It feels like the knot is a creative or intuitive or emotional or inspirational thing. It's not. There's a point of logic in there somewhere. You have to probe at it, ask questions about it, until you find it. The last point at which I was stuck in my present book, I went for a run, during which I remembered that I was trying to write a character-driven book and the one question I hadn't asked was "What did the characters want at that time?"

    I asked. I answered. I wrote on.

8. The next time I got stuck it was because I had not done the research that I normally do before starting a book. So I stopped and pursued the research. Which brought me, incidentally, to the ideas expressed in the chapter called Procedure, since what I didn't know, because I hadn't done my homework, was the procedure.

9. Go back to your outline. Expand each point. Add details.

CHAPTER 25

Writing Teachers/ Writing Books

Can a wannabe writer learn anything from writing teachers or books on writing? Or is it better to throw out the books and simply do it?

> *I've heard this notion before many times, and all I can say is that if we took that attitude toward aircraft maintenance, there'd be 747s falling out of the sky like hailstones.*
> Steve Womack, Edgar Award winner

I am a "self-taught" writer. That is to say, I didn't learn how to write by reading a book like this one or by taking creative writing courses in college or going to writers' colonies. I read a lot and the writers I read taught me by example.

We all have our favorites, but the writers I learned the most from are George Bernard Shaw, Bertolt Brecht, Joseph

Wambaugh, George Higgins, Dashiell Hammett, John D. MacDonald, Donald Westlake (especially as Richard Stark), Dick Francis, Gerald Seymour, Tom Wolfe, John Le Carré, and Eric Ambler. That's off the top of my head, in no particular order, and I missed a lot of people. When I write I try to write a book I would like to read. That is to say, I try to imitate or, as we say in polite society, emulate.

If anyone cares, in my first book I was doing a contemporary version of the classic Hammett, Macdonald & MacDonald hard-boiled. My second book was inspired by E. L. Doctorow's *Ragtime*, a historical novel that blended large, real events with the smaller actions of fictional people. *Ragtime* was set in 1896. *You Get What You Pay For*, written in 1988, was set in 1984. In *Foreign Exchange* I was emulating Eric Ambler, writing about a small person caught up in the big tides of international affairs.

Learning by reading is a terrific and lazy way to learn. Effortless, really. Thought is only painful when you're cramming, trying to figure out a year's worth of understanding in an afternoon. But if you happen to think about why you liked what you liked so much and how the writers achieved the effects that affected you, while it's going on, by the time you get to trying to do it yourself, you should have a load of techniques and tricks and approaches standing by. And, of course, you can read how-to-write books and presumably they'll have a list of the ideas that came to other people while they were reading. And while they were writing.

Here's a list of tricks I learned and where they came from.

Lawrence Block, just as Raymond Chandler did, compares Hammett to Hemingway. Virtually every sentence in *The Maltese Falcon* is an action. Every piece of dialogue is an action.

Part of this effect is achieved because Hammett never

enters the minds of any of the characters. The narrator is a camera. If someone tells a lie, Hammett doesn't tell you that it's an untruth, he just shows you how it was told. There is a great deal of description of facial expressions, of gestures and of how things are said: "He moved his shoulders wearily," "She looked at him with worried brown eyes and asked . . ." "He bawled into her frightened face." Plenty of adverbs and adjectives, but virtually no metaphors and no similes.

I learned to write dialogue from George Higgins.

Joseph Wambaugh brought reality to the police novel. No one had ever told me about being a cop the way that he does, and no one has surpassed him. He is also a brilliant black humorist, and I learned a lot about comedy from him.

Though it's somewhat less visible and less obvious, Hammett, Higgins, Francis, Shaw, Le Carré, and Ambler are also masters of their milieus. When you read these people you feel you know more about their world than the natives do. Gerald Seymour gives me that feeling when he writes about Ireland—*Harry's Game* is a classic. Some of these people are what they wrote or were very close to it: Hammett was a detective, Francis was a jockey, Le Carré was in the intelligence service, Seymour was a journalist, Shaw was part of a social set and the people of his plays are very much of that set, and Wambaugh was a cop. However, Martin Cruz Smith wrote the very convincing *Gorky Park* without even having been there for more than a couple of weeks. What is even more remarkable is that although I had a conversation with a group of Russian writers who spoke of *Gorky Park* with disdain and called it "very primitive" in its understanding of Russia, incorrect in many, many details—I am still, against the evidence of expert eyewitnesses, convinced by Smith's version of Russia. This at least suggests that it is possible to give the appearance of being a master of the milieu without being one. It's a hell of a trick.

Day of the Jackal, by Frederick Forsyth, is another hell of a trick. The conventional wisdom is, heroes have to be good guys, and if you know how it comes out, you lose the tension. Forsyth's story is about an attempt to assassinate Charles de Gaulle. The protagonist is the assassin. Worse, at the time de Gaulle was very much alive and in the news almost daily. In essence, the reader knew how the book ended. The issues were, *how* was he going to do it and *how* would he be stopped. It worked. The lesson was that it can be the process itself that is fascinating.

My tastes in the genre, for the most part, are unsuperhero. Ian Fleming, Robert Parker, Robert Ludlum, are not among my influences. Though I must say I learned one wonderful and indispensable trick from the James Bond novels—lists of brand names to create the illusion of verisimilitude. You can imitate this by getting hold of *GQ* and *Vanity Fair* and then copying the names of the most expensive liquors, perfumes, clothes, cars, vacation spots, and restaurants. From the ads; don't bother with the articles.

I picked up the trick of layering from Le Carré. He has characters tell little stories that echo the main story in both substance and style. This doesn't mean that lots of other writers haven't done it, it's just where I noticed the technique.

The idea of using footnotes, which I did rather tentatively in my first book—two or three—and extensively in *American Hero*—128 of them—came, I think, from an old Len Deighton novel.

There are a lot of references to other books throughout this book. Presumably if you want to write mysteries, it is because you love mysteries, which means you've read a lot of them. If it's not what you love and you have not read hundreds, you should write something else. I don't mean to be rude. I mean to say that if it's romance novels you spend your nights with or television you spend your life with, that's what you should be writing because that's what you know and love.

Can You Write a Book Following These Instructions?

Can you build a doghouse from a "How to Build a Doghouse" book? Install your own electrical system? Build your own dome house? Fix your marriage? Have love and a career, too!? I would like to think the answer to all of the above is a resounding "Yes, sir!!!"

I think that if you're willing to work as long and as hard as you would have to work to build your own house—for example—but not so long as it would take to have love and a career, too, you probably can.

And *heeeere's how!*

To begin we need to pick some thing, or things, for the book to be about.

It could be a caper. "Stealing the Emperor's Treasure from Japan." This has lots of possibilities. No one has ever done a Japanese caper book that I know of. So it would involve lots of exotic information. It's got automatic high tension, after all; the emperor is sacred, so his stuff probably is sacred, too.

Or it could be something you read about in the newspaper. Like the Ray Donovan story. Or a crack gang taking over an apartment building. Or a notorious murder case like the one that Dominick Dunne used for *The Two Mrs. Grenvilles*. A shorter, deadlier version of the tale is recounted by Truman Capote as a bit in *Unanswered Prayers*, an unfinished novel.

For this demonstration let us begin with theft. To lift a John D. MacDonald story, as someone did a few years ago, is poor theft. Although it got the writer published, it also got him caught and severely chastised. And it was stealing the wrong thing. What you want to do is steal something that, by your use, will be transformed. Let's take a nice rich *noir* sort of story, *Othello*, and update it. The period is so distant that simply by making it contemporary, the story automatically goes through a total revision.

After I picked it, I looked it up in INFODESK™, the small encyclopedia loaded into my computer, and I was delighted to find this: "Othello (1604), 5-act tragedy by William Shakespeare, from Giovanni Battista Giraldi's (called Cynthio) *Il Moro de Venezia*." Then this: "It was also the basis for an opera by Giuseppe Verdi (1887)." Stolen and restolen. The damn thing had been lifted as often as the Maltese Falcon. What a relief.

First, the story, because, after all, that's what, in this case, we're stealing. And the reason we're doing it is to make our life easier, give us a quick and easy template for the job we're about to do.

Othello, a noble Moor in the service of Venice, marries Desdemona and sails to Cyprus, followed by Roderigo, who loves Desdemona. Iago, who hates Othello for appointing Cassio as his lieutenant instead of

Iago, resolves to kindle Othello's suspicions by suggesting that Desdemona and Cassio are overly familiar. He also has his wife, Emilia, steal a handkerchief Othello gave Desdemona and put it in Cassio's room. When Othello sees Cassio with the handkerchief and is told by Iago that Cassio has confessed to having an affair with Desdemona, Othello resolves to kill the lovers. He gets Roderigo to kill Cassio, but he only wounds him; Iago then kills Roderigo. Othello smothers Desdemona in her bed. Emilia enters the room and Othello confesses and mentions the handkerchief. When Emilia declares she had given the handkerchief to Iago, Othello lunges at him. Iago kills Emilia and flees, is captured and brought back. Othello stabs him, then kills himself and dies upon the body of Desdemona.

INFODESK™

We will update it phrase by phrase: A *noble Moor in the service of Venice.* He will be in the service of the U.S.A., not Venice. Othello is always portrayed as black, and referred to as black in the text, although Moors, a designation no longer current, aren't black. They are a "nomadic people of North Africa of Berber and Arabic stock." Berbers are "Caucasoid African people." *Arabic* is a broad and vague expression, more a linguistic than racial designation, but refers primarily to Caucasoid people of the Middle East and North Africa. Swarthy at the most.

Nonetheless, because it is dramatic, let's go with black in the American sense of anyone who has any visible Negroid features, now called African-American.

Also, since we just had General Colin Powell, an African-American, as chairman of the Joint Chiefs of Staff, the highest military man in the nation, as Othello was in Venice, the situation has both resonance and plausibility. As a matter of

shorthand, to put an image, an idea, and a collection of characteristics in our head, let's even call the character, for now,
Omar Bradley Powell. Later on, with a couple of keystrokes,
if we find something we like better, we can change it. This
assumes you're working on a computer with a program that
has a find-and-replace function. If you're typing on a real
typewriter, or writing longhand, find another name now.

Next, let us find a Desdemona. Should she be white or
African-American? Clearly there's more drama if she is
white. Now, when we blend the story with the times, we
come up with something interesting. Beyond a certain point,
military advancement is a very, very political process. An ambitious African-American officer would not get very far with
a white wife. He almost must have an African-American wife.
Nor can he have been a bachelor; the army is suspicious of
the unmarried.

So let's make Omar B. Powell a widower. His first wife was
African-American, she was much loved, died of something.
That makes him much more of a good guy than if he'd divorced her. He has children. Three would be nice; it speaks
of a combination of potency and restraint.

After a decent period of mourning, he meets Desdemona.
Name to be changed later. Young, white, beautiful. A passionate older man/younger woman infatuation, a lust, a love.

[I swear before God, and I can produce witnesses, that
I wrote this before O. J. Simpson was on trial for killing
his wife.

The second biggest regret in my entire life is that I did not
take my own advice and write this story as a book. The first is
that back in 1976 I could have bought a full-length black
cashmere overcoat at the Shannon Airport duty-free shop for
one hundred dollars and I didn't.]

• • •

These simple first steps have designated the world we will explore, the landscape we are going to view from our train window. It is the world, primarily, of the professional military man. Not too much of it has been done, but there is a definite audience, overlapping the circles of the W. E. B. Griffith and Tom Clancy markets.

Having attempted a Clancy imitation—*Foreign Exchange* was originally going to be part techno-babble-thriller—I can testify that this is not easy material to master. Clancy was and is the ultimate high-tech buff. Griffith is a serious military buff. That is to say, many, many years of nondirect research have been loaded into the hard drives of their brains, ready to access when they write. While this is not a high-tech book, it is a military one, and stuffing yourself with that much material in a short time may not be feasible and you may not care enough to make the effort.

But for the purpose of this exercise, let's say you're an armed forces brat, your father was a colonel or your mother is a major, and you'd love to put a bunch of military types and officer corps machinations in a novel. Or you've been a reporter for a paper in a town where the military base is the biggest employer around, so you've done a bunch of stories about the military, you have some friends there, you talk the talk, know the jargon, and think you have enough insider feel to at least get started and then fill in the gaps as you need them.

Or you really, really believe in the idea. And you're willing to make the sort of major research commitment that Justin Scott did for *Ship Killer*. Not necessarily the thing to do for a first book. Justin points out that he had written four published and at least three unpublished books and he was ready, as a writer, to deal with something that size.

Let us return to the first sentence of the summary: *Marries Desdemona*. Let's make this scene a bit like that great opening wedding scene of the *Godfather*. Not in any great detail, but in its splendor and celebration, its gathering of widely different people from across the social spectrum, many of them with their own agendas, important ones, matters of ambition and power, of life and death.

The marriage of a senior officer is a major event, rich with social, emotional, hierarchical, and political relationships. Desdemona herself is a daughter of the doge, the chief magistrate, of Venice. Of course, we update that. We could make her father a federal judge or a senator. In any case, a WASP, a member of the establishment, wealthy and influential. Now we have a real powerhouse of a wedding.

What an interesting, contrasting collection of people. Her family, white and wealthy. His family, African-American, and of blue-collar background. Though his mother might well have been a schoolteacher. Her friends, young, civilian, well-to-do. His friends, mature, middle-aged, military.

We will take all the major characters and make brief sketches of them. The most prominent feature of each sketch is what they want to achieve. Their driving force. Their narrative drive. Then we will find ways to match these into the story.

The most prominent of the groom's party would be Iago and Cassio, both full colonels or perhaps even brigadier generals. I see Iago as older, Cassio as young. One is black, one is white. That could go either way.

Iago could be black. That would give him and Powell a special bond, two successful blacks in a European-American world. In many ways Iago is Omar B. Powell's closest associate, even his closest friend. Yet Omar has promoted Cassio, a European-American, over him. He's picked Cassio on merit. This is intolerable to Iago. On top of the universal reactions of jealousy and disappointment, Iago feels that Omar has betrayed both their friendship and their race.

Or Iago could be white, though nonetheless an old and trusted friend. This way he could feel that Cassio, black, was promoted only because of his race, some personal affirmative action, and therefore he could justify his jealous hatred on the basis that Omar had betrayed their friendship and the ideals of fairness and meritocracy.

Both ways have tremendous potential.

Along with the career army officers, we have the officers' wives, Emilia, Iago's spouse, chief among them. She's the same race as her husband. Again, either way, her race will be something she plays on to get close to Desdemona. If she's white, she plays on their mutuality of culture. If she's black, she plays at helping the new bride to understand black culture and the black man.

Now we have to explore the relationship between Desdemona and Cassio. Is there something between them? If so, what? Just because she was innocent in Venice doesn't make her chaste in America. Though she might be. The choices range from genuine and full fidelity, through friendship, to flirtation, all the way to the passions of consummation. Whatever we decide, we should have ambiguous hints of it here, at the wedding.

The fourth important man is Roderigo. Again, we have lots of choices to make. Young or old, black or white, soldier or civilian. Officer, noncommissioned officer, or enlisted man. My instinct, at this time, says sergeant, combat veteran, highly decorated, relatively young. Fanatically loyal to Powell, passionately in love with Desdemona and completely suppressing it. This could change later on.

There are other things that we would like to have happen at the wedding. Scenes that build up Omar B. Powell's greatness, possibly discussion of his political future. In fact, we might steal a device from *Casablanca* and from the wedding scene in *The Godfather*. We don't see the central character for a long time. We hear about him. Other people talk about him, his impressive past, about what they expect of him in the future and of what they want from him. The father-in-law has overcome his misgivings and now is speculating on the advantages of this new alliance. By the time Powell appears, we have a strong image of who he is. As we did with Rick and with Don Corleone.

There should be some girl-girl scenes between the young bride and her friends, titillating to them and to us. There should be speculation and anticipation of what her married life will be like.

We could see women of Desdemona's age flirting with young and handsome soldiers. Perhaps even more than flirting. At this point, Omar would be amused by it, but watching the heat generated by attractive young people plants a seed that will turn into poison fruit later on.

You should make a list of your favorite army stories. About promotions won and denied. About mistakes overcome and errors that ruined careers. About combat and male bonding and fear. Some will be "back story," stuff that happened in the past that formed people and motivates them still; some will be material for incidents in the oncoming story. Some will be important, some will be minor.

You should also know the history of blacks in the military. All the black officers will be familiar with those histories. Black soldiers in the Civil War, the Tuskegee Airmen, the Red Ball Express, Truman desegregating the army, who the first black officer to command white troops was, who the first black general was.

Make a list of every variation and shade of racial attitude you can think of, then scatter those attitudes, like confetti, almost at random across your list of characters. Some of the correlations won't work, some will be exciting surprises.

You should have a second set of stories about cheating wives and jealousy. These shouldn't all be melodramatic betrayals that end in blood. Some of them should be comic, some should be bawdy, some sane, and some sweet.

Now we have characters. We have a lot of material that we can use. We have a gorgeous, bang-up opening scene with military bands; an arch of raised swords for the bride and groom to walk under; stalwart, fit, and handsome young men in uniform; young, wealthy, bright-eyed women; and gaiety, drinking, open lusts, suppressed passion, plotting ambition, calculating envy.

The story structure:

We *can* tell it pretty much as Shakespeare laid it out. But we don't have to. We can borrow a completely different structure and handle the story a completely different way.

If we want a classic mystery structure, we can have Desdemona die and have an army investigator come in to find out whodunit. Perhaps you would have a two-person investigator team, in the style of Nelson DeMille's *The General's Daughter*. A black woman and a white man. They would have two radically different reactions to almost every aspect of the situation. They might, or might not, be lovers themselves. Or want to be lovers and not be able to cross their own personal racial barriers.

Or, if you like legal thrillers, you could start the book with the body being found. A brief investigation leads quickly and inexorably to the general's door. He is charged. He is put on trial.

It turns into the trial of the century, with every aspect of the criminal justice system and American society, especially the racial divide, thrown into question. It is more powerful yet if Omar Powell had been spoken of as a potential presidential candidate, one who could at last heal the racial wounds of America.

The narrator could be a black prosecuting attorney. An anti-affirmative-action Republican. That would be the movie-of-the-week choice. Or the prosecutor could be a white racist who is delighted because this proves that they are that way and no matter how you paint 'em, it's gonna come out. But he has to mask that aspect of himself. Or the narrator could be the defense lawyer: Jewish, ex-radical, ex-hippie, gone avaricious in recent years, looking to redeem himself with a cause. It could be the judge. And he has a secret.

And so on.

I really believe it is possible to make a book out of anything.

It is just a matter of formulation. A book is a story about the journey from here to there.

To make any journey requires effort, direction, forward energy. Determine what condition will create that forward motion. Then think of the obstacles that will keep the hero or heroine from reaching the goal. Make a list. Make them interesting. Line them up in order of logical necessity and dramatic significance. Figure out how the hero gets past each obstacle. Each solution must lead him to the next obstacle.

When the solutions bore you, find more interesting ones or make the obstacles tougher. If the writing isn't clear, work on it until it is. If you're not sure, show it to people who will tell you when it's confused or muddy. If it doesn't have impact, realize that the structure of storytelling is a constant process of setup and payoff, rather like a joke.

Test the dialogue by reading it out loud. Change it until it comes trippingly off the tongue. If you can't do that, find actor friends who will. Make charts and lists to keep track of your characters and the plot. If you run out of material, do research.

On a certain level, it's great fun. It's certainly as difficult and tricky as any good sport, baseball, tennis, skiing, soccer, golf.

As with any sort of construction, when you're done, you have something concrete that you can look at and hold and say, "Look at this thing. I made it." If you're reasonably good at it, you can sell it.

Sometimes it's hard, exhausting work. Fear and failure and disappointment come visiting. Still, it's better than working for a living.

DION OGUST

ABOUT THE AUTHOR

LARRY BEINHART is an internationally famous author, teacher, and lecturer on mystery and crime writing. He has conducted seminars and held fellowships at universities all over the world.

Mr. Beinhart is the Edgar Award–winning author of *No One Rides for Free*. His novels *You Get What You Pay For*, *Foreign Exchange*, and *American Hero* were published to wide critical acclaim. He has also won the Crime Writers Association's Gold Dagger and the Raymond Chandler/Fulbright fellowships.

He lives in Oxford, England, with his wife, Gillian Farrell, an actress, private eye, and writer, and their two children.